Pastoring Multiple Parishes

OTHER BOOKS IN THE
EMERGING MODELS OF PASTORAL
LEADERSHIP SERIES

Shaping Catholic Parishes:
Pastoral Leaders in the 21st Century
edited by Carole Ganim

Parish Life Coordinators:
Profile of an Emerging Ministry
by Kathy Hendricks

Pastoring Multiple Parishes

AN EMERGING MODEL OF PASTORAL LEADERSHIP

Mark Mogilka and Kate Wiskus

◇◇◇

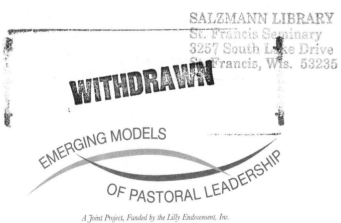

EMERGING MODELS
OF PASTORAL LEADERSHIP

A Joint Project, Funded by the Lilly Endowment, Inc.

LOYOLAPRESS.
A JESUIT MINISTRY
Chicago

Partnering for Pastoral Excellence

National Association for Lay Ministry

Conference for Pastoral Planning and Council Development

National Association of Church Personnel Administrators

National Association of Diaconate Directors

National Catholic Young Adult Ministry Association
NCYAMA

National Federation of Priests Councils

LOYOLA PRESS.
A JESUIT MINISTRY

3441 N. Ashland Avenue
Chicago, Illinois 60657
(800) 621-1008
www.loyolapress.com

Cover design by Kathryn Seckman Kirsch
Interior design by Maggie Hong

Library of Congress Cataloging-in-Publication Data
Mogilka, Mark.
  Pastoring multiple parishes : an emerging model of pastoral leadership /
Mark Mogilka and Kate Wiskus.
    p. cm.
  Includes bibliographical references.
  ISBN-13: 978-0-8294-2649-6
  ISBN-10: 0-8294-2649-3
  1. Pastoral theology—Catholic Church. 2. Parishes—United States. I.
Wiskus, Kate. II. Title.
  BX1913.M58 2009
  253—dc22

2008051861

Printed in the United States of America
09 10 11 12 13 Bang 10 9 8 7 6 5 4 3 2 1

Contents

Introduction

If you are reading this book, chances are extremely high that you minister in a multiple-parish setting or are a member of a parish that shares a pastor and/or staff with at least one other parish. We have worked in many such settings, and we have seen the need for resources and support for those in multiple-parish ministries. This book presents what we know.

◇◇◇

MARK

As the director of pastoral planning for the diocese of Green Bay for the past fifteen years, I have facilitated the linkage, merger, clustering, or closing of well over 100 parishes. Since 2004, I have had the privilege of chairing a national study committee on multiple-parish pastoring through the Emerging Models of Pastoral Leadership Project. At least once a week, I receive a phone call or e-mail that usually starts out something like this: "I heard that you are a person who knows something about multiple-parish ministries."

The calls come from the following people:

- *A member of an interparish pastoral planning committee that is thinking about either starting a multiple-parish ministry or continuing one.*
- *A pastor or parish life coordinator who either has responsibility for multiple parishes or will soon be assigned that responsibility.*
- *A member of the pastoral staff or council that shares a pastor or parish life coordinator with another parish.*
- *A member of the diocesan staff, diocesan planning committee, or priest personnel board who is trying to address the challenges of having fewer priests and is exploring options for the future.*

After they identify themselves and their roles, they conclude, "I (we) need help. What can you tell us?"

First, I invite them to tell me their stories, and I listen carefully. I learned long ago that each story and situation is unique. There is no "ideal model" when it comes to making the best of the multiple-parish ministry situation. I might ask a few clarifying questions. Then I respond. I offer a few words of encouragement and send them copies of the handouts and information I have. This is only a small part of the information gathered in recent years about multiple-parish pastoring. Following the contact, I am left feeling that I wish I had more time to talk and more written information that I could share.

◇◇◇

KATE

I have worked as the diocesan director of pastoral services, helping clergy and laity implement the diocesan strategic plan for parish pastoral staffing and seeing firsthand the impact of linking parishes with a shared pastor on both the ministers and those to whom they minister. I have seen the toll that the multiplication of masses, meetings, miles, and ministries has taken on the pastor, spending hours on the phone, speaking with parishioners who called out of anger or concern. Some situations turned out better than others. I came to see that success depended not only on the pastor's skills, but also on an informed and engaged laity. I came to appreciate the role of the diocesan offices and staff in facilitating the changes called for by a decreasing number of priests available for the pastoral care of the faithful.

I undertook doctor of ministry studies to equip myself to better assist those in ministry, most especially those involved in this process of pastoral change. For my doctoral thesis project I chose multiple-parish ministries and designed a study that gathered together pastors of multiple parishes for prayer, fraternity, and theological reflection on their experiences. I was privileged to listen in as those pastors recounted the challenges and the rewards of multiple-parish ministries.

Now as a member of the faculty at Mundelein Seminary, I hear seminarians speaking about their dioceses and the number of priests who are pastoring multiple parishes. They are concerned, because they know they will be assigned as pastors sooner than priests who were ordained twenty years ago. They know that the chances are quite high that their first assignment will be as a pastor to multiple parishes.

If you identify with any of the aforementioned groups of people, then we hope that this book will be helpful to you. In these pages, you will find a helpful collection of information that includes the current research on the topic of multiple-parish pastoring and ministry; stories of pastors, parish life coordinators, staff members, lay leaders, and parishioners; best practices in multiple-parish ministry; and practical advice for those entering this ministry or looking for ways to make the ministry more effective.

◇◇◇

The Emerging Models of Pastoral Leadership Project

Across the country, we are witnessing the emergence of new models of pastoral care and leadership. Recognizing this, six national ministerial organizations joined forces for the Emerging Models of Pastoral Leadership Project.[1] The guiding principle of the project is the belief that the life of the Catholic Church in the U.S. today depends on sustained collaboration, through the guidance of the Holy Spirit, at all levels. The project leaders envision a future characterized by collaborative, competent, and mission-focused pastors in service to parish communities nationwide. From within this group, ministerial organizations identified primary models of pastoral leadership that warranted further research, reflection, and the development of resources for the task.

The Multiple Parish Pastoring Project, a collaborative effort of the Conference for Pastoral Planning and Council Development (CPPCD) and the National Federation of Priests' Councils (NFPC), is one of those projects. It is designed to gather the best minds, data, and information available on multiple-parish ministries from researchers, diocesan leaders, and pastors of multiple parishes. This book is the culmination of almost five years of work through the Multiple Parish Pastoring Project, including three major research and data gathering components. Besides the obvious reliance upon our own experiences with this ministry and the current research and studies in the field, this book draws primarily on three sources: (1) study reports; (2) a national symposium; (3) pilot training programs dialogue.

1. *Study Reports:* The Multiple Parish Pastoring Project studied various aspects of multiple-parish ministries. These studies resulted in the following reports:

   Multiple-Parish Pastoring: Today's Realities and Tomorrow's Challenges (2005). This report represents the findings of a national survey of Catholic dioceses on diocesan policies and procedures related to ministering in multiple-parish situations, as well as the extent to which multiple-parish pastoring is occurring.[2] The survey yielded both advice for successful multiple-parish pastors and the criteria for determining who would be a successful multiple-parish pastor. Finally, the report revealed a dearth of training for multiple-parish ministries.

   Best Practices Regarding Multiple-Parish Pastoring (2006). This report provided a synthesis of written survey responses and phone interviews, involving forty-two pastors identified by dioceses in the earlier national survey. The study included all types of multiple-parish pastoring situations: the rural and urban, large and small, parishes across the street from one another and those that covered up to a 600-square-mile area.[3]

Interparochial Pastoral Councils: An Emerging Model for Parish Consultative Bodies (2007).[4] This report contained the preliminary study of interparochial pastoral councils. Research was gathered through in-depth interviews with pastors ministering in more than one parish. Pastors were chosen randomly, drawn from three national samples of parishes identified as sharing a pastor, and were stratified by region.

2. *Multiple Parish Pastoring Symposium* (2006). In February 2006, the project committee hosted an invitational symposium, *Multiple Parish Pastoring in the Catholic Church in the United States*, at the University of St. Mary of the Lake in Mundelein, Illinois. Forty-five participants gathered, including pastors of multiple parishes, diocesan pastoral planners, researchers in the field, and representatives from national ministry organizations. The symposium proceedings added greatly to the project members' understanding of the scope of multiple-parish ministries, along with its challenges and rewards. It also illuminated the need for the development of training for this ministry. Participants helped to develop indicators of excellence for the various components of multiple-parish ministry, most especially the role of pastor.[5]

3. *Multiple Parish Pastoring Pilot Training Programs* (2006). Two pilot sessions were held in the fall of 2006 with a total of 400 participants.[6] The goals of the training

pilots were threefold: to provide training, resources and networking opportunities to participants; to collect and share information and experience on multiple-parish pastoring; and to develop a greater understanding of the needs of the ministers and the parishioners involved in multiple-parish situations. Input from attendees was collected and made available for this book.

The Concluding Book

This book brings to bear all that has been gleaned throughout the Multiple Parish Pastoring Project for those engaged in multiple-parish ministries, most especially the pastors of multiple parishes. In keeping with the foundational goals of the Emerging Models of Pastoral Leadership Project, this book is designed to bring together much needed research, theological reflection, and practical strategies for furthering the mission of Christ and his Church through "collaborative, competent, and mission-focused pastoral leadership."[7] Through its pages, we hope to disseminate the valuable wisdom and insights gleaned through this project, giving space and time to theological reflection on the issues at hand. Information from each of the project components will be reported through the development of related topics.

We begin by setting the context within the first chapter, introducing the situation of fewer priests and its impact on pastoral ministry in the Church in the United States. We examine the various strategies being used to provide pastoral care for the faithful in parishes across the county, focusing on the assignment of pastors to multiple-parish ministries.

Next, in chapter 2, we present a proactive approach to managing the process involved in assisting parish leadership, parish staff, and parishioners in this transition. Specific information is given to help deal with the grief and loss initially operative within faith communities transitioning into the sharing of a pastor. Focus is placed on the willingness of the parish staffs and lay leadership of the communities to engage in planning processes that are open to the guidance of the Spirit.

In chapter 3, we focus on the role and responsibilities of the pastor of multiple parishes. We center on the pastor's primary roles and responsibilities that flow from the mission of Christ as priest, prophet, and king. Openness to the guidance of the Holy Spirit and the engagement and empowerment of the laity is stressed. In chapter 4, we identify the skills needed by pastors responsible for multiple-parish ministries, with a focus on collaborative skills.

The parish staff is addressed in chapter 5. We concentrate on the support and engagement of the pastoral staff in multiple-parish ministries situations. Relationships between the identified pastor and the pastoral staff are delineated.

Chapter 6 presents six basic models for multiple-parish ministries. Here, the emphasis is on the need for collaborative planning and openness to the development of a model best suited to the discerned needs of the parishes and parishioners being served.

In chapter 7, we identify traits that exemplify healthy multiple-parish collaboration. In chapter 8, which is on "best practices," we provide examples of how pastors in multiple-parish pastoral situations have successfully negotiated the transition.

Finally, in chapter 9, we try to answer the question of "so what?" by assessing the impact of the multiple-parish pastoral situations in the United States Church, as well as the concerns and possibilities for the future.

The situations we offer as examples are true in substance; however, certain details and characters have been changed to maintain their representative character without naming specific individuals. The situations are based on our experiences with multiple-parish ministers over the past fifteen years, as well as current research and the findings of the Multiple-Parish Pastoring Project.

There is one important caveat: we want to make it clear that we do not see multiple-parish pastoring as the ideal. However, it is a viable option currently being used to provide for the pastoral care of the faithful in the U.S. today. The ideal is still one pastor per parish as stated in Canon 526 §1: *A pastor is to have the parochial care of only one parish; nevertheless, because of a lack of priests or other circumstances, the care of several neighboring parishes can be entrusted to the same pastor.*[8] We must all continue to pray and work for vocations to the priesthood. At the same time, we must all pray and work for those who have undertaken ministry to multiple parishes, so that they may succeed in their pastoral efforts to serve Christ and his Church.

Terms

Following are terms that are used in this book and their implied meaning.

Pastor: This term represents the parish pastor. We recognize that the term "pastor" is reserved for the ordained minister who, under the authority of the bishop, is entrusted with the care of a faith community. This project's primary concern is the pastor assigned to the ministry of multiple parishes simultaneously. Material contained within this book may, however, be applicable to parish life coordinators (deacons, religious, and laity) and administrators who are entrusted with the pastoral care of multiple faith communities.

Parish: This term will be used to represent all existing faith communities, regardless of their canonical status as parish, mission, or pastoral center. The size of the faith community and its financial resources are not always indicative of the ministerial load involved in providing pastoral care to its members and overseeing the use of its resources. Likewise, the canonical terms used to describe the status of faith communities can detract from a full understanding of the expectations and hopes of its faithful.

Linked: This term will be used when addressing parishes sharing a pastor. It will take the place of terms used nationwide to designate degrees of collaboration and cooperation with shared ministers. This term will be used in the place of such describers as clustered, affiliated, associated, combined, coupled, paired, twinned, yoked, co-parishes, sister parishes, and mission of parishes. The reasoning behind the adoption of this term is that it implies relationship. Furthermore, it is the most commonly used term.

Abbreviations

CARA Center for Applied Research in the Apostolate

CPPCD Conference for Pastoral Planning and Council Development

NACPA National Association of Church Personnel Administrators

NADD National Association of Diaconate Directors

NALM National Association for Lay Ministry

NCYAMA National Catholic Young Adults Ministry Association

NFPC National Federation of Priests' Councils

USCCB United States Conference of Catholic Bishops

The Context of Multiple-Parish Pastoring

MARK

We assume you are experiencing, or are about to experience, a linked parish situation. This environment has many strains, but we have found that there are viable and faith-filled ways to thrive. We want to share our experiences and the findings of the Multiple Parish Pastoring Project to help you improve your effectiveness in a life-giving way.

◇◇◇

KATE

We've found that everyone involved in multiple-parish ministry needs to understand the context of the situation. You need to be able to see the bigger picture in order to manage the pastoral situation effectively. Pastors of multiple parishes across the U.S. are leading thriving faith communities. Multiple-parish situations involve us all, the Catholics of the United States. We're in this together.

◇◇◇

Fr. Eric worried about his new assignment as pastor of three rural parishes. He had spent the two years since his ordination as an associate at one of the largest parishes in the diocese, one with ample staff and financial resources. He felt ill-prepared to shepherd three small faith communities through the process of a linking as the shared pastor. The parishes were strung out over a thirty-mile circuit. He would have only one paid staff person, a secretary/bookkeeper at the largest of the parishes. The other two parishes had only a handful of volunteer staff. All three communities had limited financial resources.

Fr. Eric wanted training for multiple-parish ministry, but none of the dioceses in his state offered it. How would he manage? The diocesan director of pastoral services recommended that he contact a neighboring pastor who also pastored three parishes.

The diocesan director had also facilitated the initial linkage meetings with all the parishes involved, fielding the tough questions, deflecting the anger, attempting to calm the fears. Fr. Eric was grateful for that. He hoped that the anger and fear expressed by the parishioners at the preliminary meetings would abate quickly. Fr. Eric faced a multitude of questions. Parishioners wanted to know which parish would keep the prime 9 a.m. Sunday morning Mass. Which rectory would he choose for his residence? How would the parishes divide up the expenses? How could he lead them to collaboration across parish lines?

◇◇◇

Fr. Frank was a seasoned pastor. He counted his age and experience as blessings in his assignment as pastor of two large, metropolitan parishes that had been linked six years prior to his arrival. Although the running of things was relatively smooth, Fr. Frank faced many problems—primarily flowing from the complexity of big-city parish life. The two parishes had many programs, and new programs needed to be started. Immigrants were moving into the parishes. Fr. Frank was trying to learn Spanish in addition to everything else.

The archdiocese was of little help as new issues arose. The few available, written diocesan guidelines, such as those on parish councils and boards, assumed "one pastor, one parish."

There was no formal organization for peer support among pastors of multiple parishes.

Getting time away for spiritual renewal and rest proved virtually impossible. He appreciated having a good staff, but he was all too familiar with the receptionist's preface, "Father, I know you're busy, but the caller says she needs to speak to a priest now."

◇◇◇

These stories point to the complexity of the growing phenomenon of pastors of multiple parishes in the U.S. The phenomenon is nationwide. It is occurring in varying degrees in every region and state. Why is this happening now? What is behind this growing trend? Are there other ways of providing the necessary pastoral care for the faithful?

This Is Not a New Phenomenon

First, it needs to be noted that these are not entirely new stories. According to research by the Center for Applied Research in the Apostolate (CARA), there were already 549 parishes in the U. S. in 1965 (or three percent of all U.S. parishes) that did not have a resident priest.[9] This should not come as a surprise when we consider that more than half of the total area of the U.S. is classified as "home mission" territory. For many years pastors have pastored more than one parish and, for the most part, they have managed successfully.

What *is* new is the extent to which this practice has grown. In 2007, using CARA data, more than seventeen percent of the parishes in the U.S. did not have a resident priest and shared a pastor with at least one other parish.[10] Approaching the topic from a different perspective, focusing on the priest rather than the parish, Sr. Katarina Schuth looked at the number of faith communities served. Counting both parishes and missions, she placed the number that share a priest at forty-four percent in 2005.[11]

Why Is This Happening Now?

The Catholic population of the U.S. increased more than eight percent between 2000 and 2007.[12] However, during that same period, the number of priests declined eight-and-a-half percent.[13] In the past forty-plus years, the Catholic population has grown forty-eight percent and the number of priests declined by twenty-seven percent.[14] Since the number of newly ordained priests is less than the number of priests leaving active ministry because of illness, retirement, or death, this trend is not expected to reverse itself soon. In fact, forecasts predict as much as an additional twelve percent decline in U.S. diocesan priests between 2005 and 2010.[15]

For some time, sociologists have been warning about the shortage of priests and its potential impact on the Church.[16] Pastoral planners have begun to grapple with the consequences of the rising number of Catholics, the relatively static number of parishes, and the declining number of priests available for ministry.[17] Diocesan pastoral planning offices, where they exist, and vocations offices were among the first to see the trends. Diocesan priest personnel boards across the country have noted the decline. Many even undertook studies to determine the extent and pace of the decline as precursors to their strategic planning efforts.

In 2000, the United States Conference of Catholic Bishops (USCCB) published "The Study of the Impact of Fewer Priests on the Pastoral Ministry," which identified several practices being used by dioceses to deal with the immediate challenges of providing pastoral care. These were (1) closing parishes; (2) creating larger parishes; (3) appointing parish life coordinators; (4) enlisting foreign-born ministers; and (5) assigning priests as pastors to multiple parishes.[18]

The final practice, noted by the USCCB, is the fastest-growing and most frequently implemented practice nationwide.[19] We anticipate that within this first decade of our new millennium, the number of faith communities sharing a pastor will surpass fifty percent.

It must be noted that dioceses use multiple strategies simultaneously. A pastor of multiple parishes may be working with parish life coordinators, may be foreign-born or ministering with a foreign-born pastoral minister, and may be closing or merging parishes.

The Complex Reality of Multiple-Parish Ministry

The multiple-parish ministry is more complex than statistics indicate. It defies standard math, where 1+1=2. In multiple-parish ministry, 1+1=3. Pastors serving multiple parishes don't just tend to the needs of Parish A and the needs of Parish B; there are also the needs of Parish A and Parish B working collaboratively.

Each parish may have its own pastoral council. With the linking of the two, there may now also be a joint council. Parish A has a staff of two, a secretary and a religious education administrator. Parish B has a staff of three, a secretary, a religious education administrator, and a director of sacred music. But together the parishes share a youth minister. This is an example of the "multiplication factor" operative in multiple-parish ministry. With the addition of parishes, pastors often see a multiplication of Masses, meetings, miles, and ministries.

Pastors of multiple parishes must also factor in the parish schools and diocesan, or institutional, responsibilities. Of the parishes/missions included in Sr. Katarina Schuth's study, 35.7 percent had schools associated with them.[20] Some 42 percent of the priests had additional pastoral ministry responsibilities such as assignments to diocesan offices and chaplaincies.[21]

The diversity of the U.S. Church further adds to the complexity of multiple-parish ministry. Today, fewer than half of Catholic adults ages eighteen to forty are white, non-Hispanic.[22] Diversity extends beyond ethnicity to include such factors as family structures, life styles, regional migration, aging, and economic status. Parishes are called on to develop programs and ministries to serve this diverse membership.

Finally, compounding the complexity, is the collaboration called for in the 1983 Code of Canon Law. "The canons direct or imply that others—lay persons, deacons, religious, assisting priests—will work with the pastor in providing pastoral care."[23] Parishes are required to have a functioning finance council and, if deemed beneficial by the bishop of the diocese, a functioning pastoral council.

This collaborative spirit is stressed by Pope John Paul II in *Christifideles Laici*, when he writes that local ecclesial authorities should seek "adaptations of the parish structures according to the full flexibility granted by canon law, especially in promoting participation by the lay faithful in pastoral responsibilities."[24] Pope Benedict XVI speaks of "the co-responsibility of the entire parish" noting that "the parish priest is no longer the only one to animate everything."[25] No one denies that collaboration and consultation are valuable, but not everyone understands the complexity of collaborative ministry.

All of these factors complicate the situation to some degree; however, they also have the potential of benefiting both the ministers and the communities. Schools can add life to a parish. Diversity can enrich the practices of a faith community. Pastoral duties, such as chaplaincies and vocations work, can be rewarding ministerial experiences. Collaboration can energize everyone involved through the infusion of the Holy Spirit, who is at work within them and through them.

Crucial Variants Affecting the Ministry

Three important variants for pastors of multiple parishes are the number of parishes being served, their size, and their proximity to one another. The majority of multiple-parish ministries involve two parishes (seventy percent). However, the numbers can soar to six or more. The majority (eighty-five percent) of parishes sharing a pastor are small, under 500 families.[26] While just more than half of these pastors travel fewer than 500 miles monthly in the course of their pastoral ministry, forty-seven percent of the priests studied by Sr. Katarina Schuth travel more than that. Some twenty-three percent of them travel more than 1,000 miles monthly.[27]

One Final Note

Some see the issue of multiple-parish pastoring as essentially one of supply and demand. However, it should not be reduced to numbers. The issue today, as always, is the essential, ongoing mission of Christ in our world. How will we, as the Catholic Church in the U.S., further that mission in this time? The numbers need to seen in a spiritual context. How will we be his church, in relationship to him and to one another because of him? The way we are called to be church is changing. As theologian David Power, OMI, suggests, we must "promote and structure ministries that facilitate being church" in our modern time.[28]

Christ's mission and our relationship to him and one another are the heart of the matter and of this book. We use statistics to give an accurate picture of the current situation, but this book is not about statistics. Our intent is to further the mission of Christ by sharing wisdom gleaned from others, from pastors who are pastoring multiple parishes, from parishioners collaborating under the direction of a shared pastor, and from diocesan personnel supporting their efforts. The goal of the Multiple-Parish Pastoring Project[29] was to produce practical resources and materials for use by those in the field.

We intend this book to provide some hope needed by pastors of multiple parishes, as well as by those being served. In his encyclical letter *Spe Salvi*, Pope Benedict XVI writes of the power and purpose of hope:

> *Redemption is offered to us in the sense that we have been given hope, trustworthy hope, by virtue of which we can face our present: the present, even if it is arduous,*

*can be lived and accepted if it leads towards a goal,
if we can be sure of this goal, and if this goal is great
enough to justify the effort of the journey.*[30]

The "effort of the journey" is tremendous for those pastoring multiple parishes and for the staffs and members of those communities. But it must not overshadow or obliterate the great hope on the part of the pastors, staffs, and parishioners that we have witnessed and the great benefits we have seen.

2

Moving from Single- to Multiple-Parish Ministry

Moving from the traditional model of "one pastor, one parish" to the model of pastoring multiple parishes means change, not only for those in the ministry, but also for those to whom they minister. The changes impact everyone from the bishop to the person in the pew. How we handle those changes will, to a large extent, determine how well we grow as Christ's church in this place, at this time, and with these people.

◇◇◇

MARK

People often react with stunned silence to the news that their parish will be linked to another. At times this will give way to anger. Priests will often ask for help in dealing with their own resistance to their changing realities. They get right to the heart of the issue: What does it mean to be pastor of more than one parish? Do the expectations change for laity? What do I do with my own expectations of what it means to be a priest, a pastor?

A pastor shared the following reflection with me. "When I was ordained, as I looked down the road, I expected that when I hit around age 55, if I had paid my dues and was basically a good priest, I would be made pastor of a good-sized parish in the suburbs, with two or more young priest associates, and life would be very good. Then things changed. Now you reach age 55, they just give you two or more parishes, no associates, and you're not sure what to expect."

◇◇◇

KATE

Certain reactions are present in every situation of parishes sharing a pastor. The pastors are concerned. How would they manage? What advice could I give them so that they could best pastor through the transition? Some parishioners cannot believe that their parish would be without a resident pastor and others want to know why they have to share a pastor. Some are angry. Some had seen it coming and wanted to know how best to engage in the process.

It helps to focus on the parish as a faith community, rather than a "consumer," and on the priest as pastor rather than "manager." It also helps to give everyone all the information available. It helps people accept the necessity of the change and encourages all to look collaboratively for answers that are good for everyone. Of course, prayer helps, especially when it is prayer composed for and by the community.

Every situation has genuine challenges and struggles. Resistance to change is natural. Providing for those most challenged by change is imperative.

◇◇◇

What Have We Learned about Change from the Multiple-Parish Pastoring Project?

Change is inevitable, but change that evolves from consultative planning processes is usually accepted more readily than change that is perceived to have been "imposed from on high." The Multiple-Parish Pastoring Project has shown that dioceses that have anticipated the priest shortage and engaged the clergy and laity in extensive planning processes have found that the people and their pastors more successfully navigate the challenges of change. Put another way, change is easier to accept when you initiate it yourself. Change that is implemented without planning and without engaging those impacted, often results in wounds that will take generations to heal.

But even well-planned change presents challenges. Human beings naturally resist change. All systems—natural and societal—seek equilibrium and stability. Change challenges us. The apostles understood this. Account after account in the Acts of the Apostles describes the challenges the disciples and the new communities of Christians faced in the wake of the resurrection and Pentecost. We do well to understand that change dares us to anticipate those challenges and to charitably move forward together in building up the Body of Christ.

A second lesson learned through the project is that staying mission-focused helps everyone deal with change. The transition from "one pastor, one parish" to linking multiple parishes is not about what someone will gain or lose. It is about how we will be Church now, given our present gifts, resources, and limitations.

Challenges for Pastors

Pastors understandably find the transition challenging because most people see the "one pastor, one parish" model as the norm. Multiple-parish ministry is a step away from that norm. Priests must deal with changes in their priestly identity, while managing the expectations of the faithful.

Pastors are priests. Their priestly identity flows from their humanity, their discipleship, and their ministries as ordained priests.[31] Multiple-parish ministry means that they have to find a new balance among their ministries, their own discipleship, and their human needs. Questions arise. Pastors participating in the Multiple-Parish Pastoring Project have shared these questions with us. How will I manage? How will I maintain my own personal prayer and spiritual development? How will I balance my pastoral presence at multiple sites to multiple communities? Will I feel like a "circuit rider?" How will I celebrate more Masses and sacraments without becoming a "sacramental machine?" How will I balance ministry with administration? Will I have to supervise more staff? Will I have enough staff? How can I keep the administrative duties as pastors from taking away my time for the priestly ministries that give me life?

Challenges for Parishioners

The majority of the laity live out their faith in a specific place, at a specific time, with specific people. This is the context in which they enter into relationship with Jesus Christ and his church and how they celebrate and live what they believe. Parish for the laity in the U.S is a way of encountering Jesus with other like-minded people. "Parish" is personal.

When members of a parish hear that they are going to be sharing a pastor, questions immediately flood their minds. Who will we call for sacraments? When will we have Mass? Who will take care of things while Father is at the other parish? Does this mean our parish will be closed? Will Father prefer the other parish to ours? What about our parish traditions? Will we have to give up the Children's Christmas Eve Mass?

Grief can set in quickly. It manifests itself in various ways.[32] People are shocked. "How can this be happening?" "What will become of our parish?" "What will become of our school?" "Why is this happening to us?" "Why even bother? Aren't you just going to close our parish in a few years anyway?" At times, people try to bargain. "If this happens, we'll refuse to give to the diocesan appeal." "We'll only support this if the pastor lives in our rectory." They question the fairness of the process. "Why us? We have a school. Why don't you take a pastor away from the next parish without a school?" "Why did you take our pastor away and give St. Anne's an associate?" Sometimes, people will leave for another parish, reduce their contributions, or begin a letter writing campaign to the bishop.

How Can We Best Facilitate the Necessary Changes?

Here are a few things we have learned about how to best navigate the initial stages of transition to a multiple-parish pastoring model.

Pray for Discernment

The first piece of advice is to pray. We imitate Jesus, who took time for prayer and reflection. Some pastors, their staffs, and lay leaders have drafted a prayer unique to their communities, calling upon the Holy Spirit for help in discerning the right path for all involved. They use this prayer to open every meeting. They pray it together at weekend liturgy. Others have held days of prayer and reflection for the whole parish or the parish leadership, to reflect on the work that must be undertaken. Prayerful discernment through the Holy Spirit is essential. Remember, "Nothing is impossible for God."[33]

Engage Those Impacted by the Anticipated Change

Engage the people involved in the process of change as soon and as extensively as possible. The more engaged people are, the better they will be able to manage change positively. In our experience, when change seems forced from top down, with little involvement of local leaders, there is a noticeable loss of parishioners and of commitment to the local church and its leadership.

Since change involves risk and often means embarking into unknown territory, it is imperative to communicate effectively and openly. The process must be transparent and characterized by compassionate listening to individuals. This means regular bulletin reports on the progress of the process, sharing information appropriately with parish leaders, and providing a forum for anyone to ask questions. It is important to provide as much information as possible about the facts that have led to this change, any alternatives considered, and the rationale for the course taken.

Recognize Grief and Address It Compassionately

Using Jesus as our model, compassion must flow throughout the process. People can't be rushed through change. Experience has shown that they will need time to adjust, and part of this adjustment will inevitably involve grief. Communities that do not allow for grief in dealing with a change of this magnitude can hold onto their anger and division for generations. Given time and compassion, grief can give way to acceptance of and even excitement for the current reality.

A major change like this can wound a parish community. But wounds can heal if they are well cared for. In time, scar tissue can grow, leaving the site of the former wound even stronger than before. Conversely, wounds that are neglected can become infected and fester for a very long time. They may never heal correctly. Over time, they can drain life away.

Loving, gentle, and compassionate care is crucial. Pastors who fail to be sensitive to their parishioners' need to grieve the loss of their own full-time pastor risk a community unable to grow through the challenge. The wounds may fester with undercurrents of resentment and anger that can sabotage a community for generations.

Timing can be crucial. There are two schools of thought about dealing with wounds: the "get it over and move on" school and the "go slowly" school. The "get it over" approach moves quickly. It's like ripping a bandage off a healing wound, so as to not prolong the pain. The "go slowly" approach takes a lot of time. It removes the bandage slowly, a little at a time, perhaps soaking it for awhile between steps. We favor the second approach. It has the potential to keep the largest number of parishioners engaged throughout the process of change. While the first strategy can force change, it can also drive more people from the parish community than the second.

Use Ritual as a Pastoral Tool to Heal and Comfort

For a sacramental people, ritual fits naturally within the change process and accelerates healing. Michael Weldon's book, *A Struggle for Holy Ground: Reconciliation and the Rites of Parish Closure*, details the need for ritual within the grieving process of parish closure. But rituals can also be used to facilitate healing at other times, such as in the linking of parishes and the loss of a resident pastor or the merging of parishes. "The articulation of deep anger and powerlessness in a ritual context can serve to cleanse strong negative emotions and facilitate healing for a local church."[34]

Ritual can also be used to inaugurate something new and dedicate it to the glory and service of God. Pastors have scheduled "Unity Masses" with parishes being linked and sharing a pastor. At those celebrations, members of all the parishes involved gather together and participate in the commissioning of the leaders and staff of each parish as coworkers for a common mission. Afterwards, they share a meal.

Ritual is imperative when parishes are merged and a new parish is being formed. The rituals may include bringing items of special importance from each of the parishes into the new common worship space or incorporating architectural features of each church into the new church. The ritual helps to internalize the external change.

Provide for the Training of the Pastors and Lay Leaders

A key finding of the Multiple-Parish Pastoring Project was the lack of training provided for the pastor, staff, and lay leaders of the involved parishes. Training is essential for the pastor. Pastors participating in the project said that they did not receive seminary training in administration, time management, conflict management, and collaborative skills. The pastors of multiple parishes participating in the project stressed the need for training for multiple-parish ministry, especially the administrative components. Since this is new territory for parish staff and lay leaders, they also need training in navigating this transition.

Use an Outside Consultant to Facilitate Initial Dialogue and Negotiations

An outside consultant with experience facilitating organizational planning and change should be engaged to mediate the initial dialogue and planning for the linking of parishes. Some decisions need to be made at the beginning.[35] Primary among these include the new Mass schedule (Sundays, weekdays, and major feasts), the pastor's residence, and financial arrangements for shared services. The facilitator can help begin the conversation about collaboration in shared programs, ministries, and services.

Not every diocese has a planning office or pastoral services office that works with parishes during the linking processes. When a diocesan consultant is unavailable, parishes can seek a local facilitator to help with the process.

Why Is All of This So Important?

We've learned that there is no perfect solution that can be applied to every instance. The possibilities are numerous. Those parishes which are judged successful are following a particular model of ecclesiology, collaborative in nature, where the leaders and the faithful work together. Those that are succeeding have practiced patience and prudence, have communicated what is happening, and have sought consultation whenever possible. The multiple-parish situations that are thriving are those where the planning and process of transition were mission-focused.

3

Pastoral Leadership

MARK

Often, pastors of multiple parishes say something like, "Provide leadership? Gosh, we're just trying to survive here." How does one help a pastor move from the survival mode of operation to a more life-giving mission approach? It's often helpful to look at leadership, especially the unique kind of leadership required by multiple-parish pastoring.

I like a somewhat simple, two-part definition of leadership. First, it is the ability of a person or group to articulate a vision; second, it is the ability to engage a group of people to help to make that vision a reality. Both parts are needed for good leadership. Within the context of multiple-parish pastoring, there are additional components: the pastor engages the faith community in dialogue; the dialogue is informed through study and reflection on the teachings of the church; the dialogue is illuminated through personal and communal prayer to discern God's will for the community at a particular time. Once the vision is discerned, pastors engage members of the community in the use of their gifts to help make God's will a reality.

For the pastor of two or more parishes, this means discerning a vision for each individual parish and for the parishes together. It is important to engage the parishioners in this process. This is one of the key challenges and opportunities faced by pastors who serve two or more parishes.

◇◇◇

KATE

I would add one thing: the most effective pastors of multiple parishes share a sense of purpose that flows from their understanding of the mission of Jesus Christ. They share this understanding with the people they pastor. This makes risk-taking meaningful and possible for these men.

◇◇◇

Who Is Going to Lead?

The majority of multiple-parish pastoral leaders are priests assigned as either pastors or administrators. However, canon law provides for alternatives for the pastoral leadership. Specifically, Canon 517.2 states that "due to a dearth of priests, a bishop may delegate the pastoral care of a parish to a deacon or lay ecclesial minister." They account for a vital but modest number of pastoral leaders of multiple parishes. [36]

What Do We Mean by "Pastoral Leadership" within the Multiple-Parish Situation?

We have already identified leadership as 1) the ability of a person or group to articulate a vision; and, 2) the ability to engage a group of people to help make that vision a reality. Adding "pastoral" elevates simple leadership to a new and exciting level by opening it to the intervention and guidance of the Holy Spirit.

Pastoral leadership is a prayerful process, led by a pastor in dialogue with a community of faith. Together, they will study and reflect on scripture, the teachings of the Church, current theology, examples of successful parishes, and the current realities faced by the communities. Together, they discern God's will for the communities and make a plan of action that works towards the realization of the vision.

Pastors in the project identified three essential aspects of pastoral leadership in multiple-parish ministry.

- Mission-focused: Centered on the overarching reason for all we are and do as church.

- Adaptive: Discerning and naming the vision and the skill needed to realize that vision, by executing a plan of action.
- Collaborative: The ways in which members of the community are engaged in helping to make the vision a reality.

Mission-Focused

One day, Blessed Mother Teresa was tending to a person in dire physical condition, unclean and terribly ill, on a street of Calcutta. A Westerner passed by, observed her tender care of the individual, and remarked, "I wouldn't do that for a million dollars." To which she replied, "Neither would I." This is mission-focused. Focus on the mission allows leaders and followers alike to see the bigger picture. Focus on the mission, especially Christ's mission, unites the community around the pastoral leader. Finally, focus on the mission makes risk-taking possible and even meaningful. One pastor put it this way, "When I got over the initial shock and realized that this wasn't about me, I felt liberated and energized." He added, "Then I shared this with the people. I told them that it's about Christ's mission, in which we all participate through our baptism. Immediately, the dynamics of the situation changed. The people in the parishes realized that this was about building up and not tearing down. This wasn't something being done to them any longer. Suddenly this was something they were doing *together*."

Another pastor shared his experience. "The parishes were at odds with one another. We were really struggling initially.

Then, at the meeting of all three parish councils where we decided to do a joint bulletin, someone asked if the individual parish mission statements would be on the cover, as they had been when each parish had its own bulletin. As a group, we looked at the statements and saw their similarity because, of course, they were based on the overarching mission of Christ. Suddenly, we found our common ground—Christ's mission. And things started to turn around."

Time and again, the pastors of multiple parishes pointed to the need to be mission-focused, and to insist that the processes of transition and strategies for their future be guided by the mission of Christ and the anointing of all baptized to share in that mission. All involved in the multiple-parish situation need to be invited into a loving and life-giving relationship with Christ and with one another.

Adaptive

The one certainty in the field of pastoring multiple parishes is that things are going to change. It's inevitable. Pastors must change the way they minister. They must lead the community in accepting the necessary changes and adapting to them. The transition is going to be bumpy. Pastors need to be adept at adaptive work and engaging the community in adaptive work.[37] Together, they will consider who they are and what they will do for the mission of Christ.

One pastor commented, "I thought my experience would mean everything. Then I realized that this was different. Sure, I could draw on what I'd done in the past as a pastor of a single parish, but as Dorothy said, 'Toto, we're not in Kansas anymore.' What works with one parish isn't always a good fit with three."

Another pastor, recalling the transitional period for the four parishes he pastored, said, "The biggest adjustments were for the parish members who had their own histories and traditions. I thought the first Christmas might be our last, with all the arguing over which parish got the 5 P.M. Children's Mass."

Change challenges values. One area where adaptive work has proven effective has been the pastoral care of the sick. Historically, only the pastor makes sick calls. In a linked situation this is often impossible. Lay ministers and deacons are called upon to assist with the parishes' pastoral outreach to the sick. The value upheld through this adaptive measure is the faith community's commitment to pastoral care and presence for those in need.

Canon law actually presumes adaptive work at the local level. "Parishes will in the eyes of the law differ in their application of, or emphasis upon, certain prescriptions, because the pastoral needs of each local community will differ, as well as the competencies and charisms of each community's individual leaders."[38] This is a key point for pastors of multiple parishes. It is up to the pastor and the parish to make necessary adaptations.

Canon law presumes the "one pastor, one parish" model. While it makes provisions for other models of pastoral care, it gives little direction for pastoral care in the presentation of these models. In fact, this presumption creates one of the unique challenges for the pastors of multiple parishes. Canon Law prescribes that the pastoral care entrusted to the pastor is to be personal, as "a shepherd who truly knows his flock." It further notes that pastors should visit families and develop personal relationships with them. While most pastors would love to be able to develop personal, pastoral relationships with each member of the communities they serve, they need to get on to the next parish for Mass. Does adaptive work mandate the entrusting of certain aspects of pastoral presence to others in the parish? The "one pastor, one parish" presumption is carried over into pastoral guidelines, statements, pastoral letters, and programs issued by the Vatican, the USCCB, local bishops, and diocesan offices. Pastors of multiple parishes read these materials and are left with questions. "Does this apply to me?" "How can I live the spirit of this pastoral guideline in a multiple-parish setting?"

For example, the pastor gets a copy of the diocesan guidelines for parish finance councils which notes that the pastor should be present for every meeting of the council because the work is so important. What if the pastor has three or more parishes that are geographically distant? Is attendance at all these meetings the best use of the gifts and talents of the pastor? Can a pastor delegate a staff member to represent him at these meetings?

Leading multiple parishes obviously necessitates adaptation. Pastors who are grappling with the question of balancing the ideal with the pastoral realities and limitations they face have noted the benefit of having a pastoral peer support group or network. They saw this support as critical. Such support provides feedback so the pastor can ensure that adaptations don't go too far. These groups offer alternatives for dealing with pastoral situations that are more in keeping with the spirit or intent of given canon laws, diocesan policies, and procedures.

The Church's international, national, and diocesan pastoral statements and guidelines need to be sensitive to these challenges and provide guidance on appropriate adaptations. In the meantime, blessed is the pastor who is adept at adaptive work.

It is appropriate to offer a story about adaptation. In the late 90s, a pastor was assigned to three parishes in a small city of 6,000. The diocese had set the ground rules: no parishes will be closed. The pastor saw his role as ministering to three separate faith communities. As he met with the separate parish leaderships, the same issues arose in each. How was each to manage with dwindling resources?

Each parish had a school building, even though the schools had been consolidated twenty-five years earlier. Each of the parishes had a convent and a rectory, even though they now shared a pastor and the religious community teachers had left long ago. Between the three parishes, there were fourteen buildings, many of which were empty and in need of repairs. The councils were wrestling with the issue of funding catechesis, pastoral care, and outreach, while facility costs were eating up most of their financial resources.

Under the new pastor's direction, the leadership of the three parishes began meeting together. Within a year, the questions were articulated. Wouldn't we be serving God and each other better if we were a united Catholic community, rather than three separate parishes? Wouldn't we be better stewards of the gifts given to us as communities if we weren't pouring all this money into heating and caring for buildings that we no longer use or need?

It took three more years for that community to convince the diocese that they wanted to be merged into one parish. It took another seven for the united Catholic community of that town to build a new parish church that incorporated features from the three original sacred structures. It wasn't an easy path, but it was one that the pastor and parish leaders had prayerfully discerned. Together, they crafted not only a vision statement, but also a prayer for the transition, which they prayed at every meeting.

This example illustrates essential elements of adaptive work: being open to the Holy Spirit's direction; discerning the events and situations through faithful eyes and with hopeful hearts; and envisioning what could and should be based on values flowing from a shared mission.

One of the key skills that pastors need when doing adaptive work is the ability to manage change. Often that means a strategy of taking two steps forward and one step back. As one pastor explained, "Sometimes when you have a big plan that may require a great deal of change, you start by running a rough proposal up the flag pole to see if it'll fly. If it does, then you move on with implementation. If it doesn't—then you've got to bring it back down and make some adjustments before you try again."

Another pastor explained his experiences with a new building proposal, which would serve all the parishes in the linkage. "You put your best into the first proposal. Make sure you note clearly the rationale, including the needs that will be addressed through the effort, and then see if you can get it passed. If it fails you pull it back, review the concerns that led to the defeat of the measure, make some adjustments, and reintroduce it again next year. If it is important enough, the needs will still be there. And if you have responded to the concerns of people in your revised proposal, it should pass the second time."

In adaptive work, the pastors are not limited by the past. They allow for experience, they consider histories, but they are ultimately concerned with the future. The pastor mentioned above, who led the initiative to merge three separate faith communities into one, articulated the sense of loss for the communities as they sacrificed their separate sacred spaces in order to realize unity. He helped them to evaluate their past and vision for their future, discerning what to hold on to and what to let go.

The adaptive part of envisioning consists of identifying the conflicts between the values of the communities and the realities they face. Envisioning allows everyone to identify the core values and beliefs of their communities and the behaviors necessary to realize those values in tangible ways. The whole community is involved in the envisioning, but the pastor will ultimately articulate it through word and example, thus mobilizing the community to make the vision a reality.

Envisioning requires discernment. By discernment, we mean the active deciphering of events and situations in light of faith. "Where is God drawing us as community?" That is the essential question. The pastor plays a critical role in discernment. "How will the bringing together of these communities draw us closer to God? What is God summoning us to do at this time? How has the Holy Spirit gifted the communities and individuals for the future of our faith?" Once the vision is discerned, the pastor can affirm, encourage, and celebrate through the grace of God what is and what will be.

Collaborative

Who is going to lead? This is not a simple question. "To lead" implies followers with some shared purpose. In this instance, those being led are the members of the multiple parishes, who share with their pastor the mission of Christ in a particular time and particular place.

In the project interviews we constantly heard "The leader is important, but the leader doesn't and shouldn't do this alone." The pastor does not do all that needs to be done for the life of the faith communities, nor is the pastor alone in the situation. In fact, Pope Benedict XVI addressed this very issue when he responded to a pastor of multiple parishes who asked how, given all the responsibilities, clergy in similar situations were to manage. The Holy Father responded:

> He should not be reduced to being mainly and above all a coordinating bureaucrat. On the contrary, he should be the one who holds the essential reins himself but can also rely on collaborators. I believe that this is one of the important and positive results of the council: the co-responsibility of the entire parish, for the parish priest is no longer the only one to animate everything. Since we all form a parish together, we must all collaborate and help so that the parish priest is not left on his own mainly as a coordinator, but truly discovers that he is a pastor who is backed up in these common tasks in which, together, the parish lives and is fulfilled.[39]

We are called to collaboration in the mission of Christ through our very baptism.[40] It is through collaboration, guided by the Spirit, that the early church flourished. In his letters, Paul focused on the Body of Christ and its collaborative dynamics. Building up the Body of Christ is no less important today than it was in Paul's time. In fact, in multiple-parish situations, modern-day pastors see collaboration as essential.

The pastors of multiple parishes define collaboration as "valuing the unique and essential work of every member." They want each member of the community to function appropriately, so that "living the truth in love, we should grow in every way into him who is the head, Christ."[41] This dynamic ecclesiology requires strong pastoral leadership that focuses the faith community on their participation in the ongoing mission of Christ and that draws everyone into full participation in that mission. Through active discipleship in a particular place and time, the vision for the parishes, prayerfully discerned, can be realized.

Canon law actually demands this collaborative ecclesiology. "Canon law presumes that the pastor will enlist the assistance of the faithful in the discharge of his responsibilities... He is expected to rely upon their counsel and to foster their participation."[42]

In the appendix, you will find a copy of a job description for pastor and parish. In workshops on multiple-parish ministry, we shared a copy of this job description and asked for comments. The almost unanimous response was incredulity: "This is overwhelming. No one person should be expected to do all this." We agree. But when we asked what should be eliminated, people said, "It all should be there, but. . . ."

The "but" is the point. The canonical expectations for pastors are overwhelming enough for the pastor of a single parish. They are more overwhelming for a pastor of multiple parishes. If it is impossible for one person to do all these things—and all of them are important—then the only way that this mission can be accomplished is by engaging all the gifts and talents of staff and parishioners. Collaboration isn't just an option, it's a requirement.

Collaboration includes consultation. Consultation with the lay leadership of the parishes and the staff of each parish is invaluable for successful navigation through the channels of transition. This is especially true initially, when the pastor and the communities must prayerfully discern a vision for each community and for the combined communities. These consultations provide direction and energy. They provide an opportunity for communities to feel ownership for the vision. Parishioners are called to generously contribute their time, talents, and treasures to help make the vision a reality. They are called into stewardship as disciples.

We have personal experience with a linked setting involving five parishes and a chapel that is an outstanding example of the benefits of consultation and collaboration. The leaders gathered for an evening of review and renewal two years after they began working together as linked parishes. One of the exercises was to name the places they had seen the hand of God at work in the last eighteen months. With a little encouragement, the groups set to work. We wrote the items on newsprint taped to the walls. We had a total of sixty-two items.

The leaders were proud, excited, and animated. They said, "I didn't know that," "Isn't it wonderful that we are doing that,"

"I had no idea we were doing that many good things," "We've accomplished more in the last eighteen months than I thought we had." But the key insight was, "We'd have never had anywhere near this many good things happening two years ago when we were five separate parishes and a chapel. But because we've come together sharing our resources, we have been able to do more collectively than we could if we'd stayed separate."

4

What Tools Can Help?
Pastoral Skills Worth Nurturing

MARK

Recent research suggests that our seminaries are doing a good job at training men to be good priests—especially in the areas of pastoral care, sacramental ministry, and the knowledge and understanding of the faith necessary for catechesis and evangelization.[43] However, we've heard from pastors of multiple parishes that the seminaries did not, as a rule, provide adequate training for modern parish administration and pastoral planning. There is also a similar gap of training for parish life coordinators appointed by bishops to provide for the pastoral care of a parish.

In the past, priests learned how to be pastors by serving as associates under-experienced pastors and parochial vicars before becoming pastors themselves. Now, priests are being appointed as pastors very soon after ordination; there is little time for them to learn how to be a good priest much less a pastor who can build and grow a parish.

As a result, new pastors may struggle and are not as effective as they might be because they lack basic leadership and administrative skills. These skills can be learned. In this chapter we discuss them.

◇◇◇

KATE

In my role as a diocesan director of pastoral services and planning, I worked closely with the pastors of multiple parishes. I learned early on that most of these pastors are dedicated to their ministry and find a great deal of satisfaction in it, a point corroborated by Sr. Katarina Schuth in her research, which showed that less than seven percent were dissatisfied with their ministry.[44] I found that the difference between pastors who were flourishing and those who were struggling was often a matter of pastoral skills. Through the Multiple-Parish Pastoring Project we have identified skills necessary for successful pastoring of multiple parishes. I agree with Mark that these skills are necessary for pastors attempting to grow the faith and the Church in their multiple-parish settings, and that time spent acquiring and honing these skills is time well spent.

Seminaries are changing. Mundelein Seminary, where I serve as faculty and associate dean of formation, has added courses in pastoral care, administration, and even in pastoring multiple parishes. These additions complement the experiences gained by the men in formation through field education, clinical pastoral experiences, and pastoral internships.

◇◇◇

Why Identify a Skill Set for Pastors of Multiple Parishes?

The obvious answer is that the position of leader requires specific skills, exercised with proficiency and efficiency. But ours is not a business culture that judges success by profits—or even numbers. Ours is a mission-driven endeavor, and the mission is not ours, but Christ's. We participate in it as disciples and ministers.

In an audience with parish priests, Pope Benedict XVI responded to a pastor of multiple parishes concerned about his effectiveness.

> *The problem in general is to ensure that, despite the new situations and new forms of responsibility, the parish priest does not forfeit his closeness to the people, his truly being in person the shepherd of this flock entrusted to him by the Lord . . . to ensure that the parish priest continues to be a pastor and does not become a holy bureaucrat.* [45]

The skills we present enable pastors to pastor, not just manage. These skills afford the pastors the means of ministry necessary for the essential tasks at hand, enabling them to grow the Church and not just maintain it.

Which Skills Did the Multiple-Parish Pastoring Project Identify as Necessary?

Through surveys, interviews, gatherings, and dialogues, the project was able to identify fifteen pastoral skills or tools necessary for effective leadership by the pastors of multiple parishes. They are

- Use of Prayer
- Transparency and Openness
- Pastoral Presence
- Collaboration
- Pastoral Planning
- Conflict Management
- Community Building
- Delegation
- Administration
- Personnel Oversight
- Fiscal Management
- Time Management
- Communication
- Stress Management
- Ministerial Self-Care

Use of Prayer

Pastors must themselves be people of prayer and leaders of prayer for the communities they shepherd. Throughout the project, participants repeatedly stressed the necessity of prayer for the communities in transition and also for the leaders themselves. Prayer is the foundation of discernment, and it sustains and stabilizes both those who minister and those served.

The pastor must model prayerfulness and must invite the community to prayer throughout the process. Prayer should sustain the processes, gatherings, ministries of the pastor, fellow ministers, and community members. It is often fitting to compose a prayer for the members of the linked parishes. This helps to achieve a common vision for their future and focuses on God's grace in the situations we face.

Pastors who successfully navigate the transition to multiple-parish situations speak of being Spirit-fed, Spirit-led, and Spirit-driven. They talk about the manifestations of the fruits of the Spirit, such as charity, joy, peace, patience, kindness, generosity, and faithfulness. Clearly, prayer is at the heart of it. As one pastor put it, "You know how they say 'on a wing and a prayer?' Well, we found out early on that the wing was optional, but the prayer was mandatory."

Transparency and Openness

Sharing involves three stages: the initial coming together, the awkward moments of becoming familiar with the new situation, and finally the camaraderie. We want to focus on that awkward middle phase.

When parishes enter into a sharing process with other parishes, a phase of suspicion usually comes fairly quickly, especially if the decision to link was not theirs. Parishioners are concerned about fairness, about equality, about getting their needs met. They're concerned about the pastor's motives or agenda. The suspicion can flow from the communities' judgment that this linkage is being done *to* them. The pastor is suspect because of his association with whoever did this to them. This situation can become even more strained when the pastor has been the pastor of one of the parishes and shares a history with that parish. The other parishes fear that there will be a favorite parish.

The antidote is transparency and openness on the part of the pastor. Transparency means sharing what you know as soon as you know it. It mandates good communication about the progress of the transition. It means stating the issues and questions openly and to all whom are affected by the process. Transparency means open meetings and frequent updates and reports in the bulletin and announcements.

Openness refers to what others know, feel, and do. Openness mandates good communication skills, such as listening to parishioners' fears. Openness requires honoring thoughts and gifts that are different from your own. Openness means that it's not "your way," but rather "the way," which will be determined collectively and prayerfully. The project symposium recommended town hall meetings to allow any and all parishioners to participate in the transitional process and to provide a forum for parishioners to articulate their feelings and concerns.[46]

In one parish, parishioners were distressed at the news of the linkage because another parish in the city had closed years before. This linkage involved a larger parish with a school and a smaller parish with no school and only one staff person. The linking pastor had already served at the larger parish for a couple of years, so parishioners of the smaller parish feared that they would be treated like a "stepchild." The pastor was astute in his handling of the situation. He reached out to the members of the smaller parish and to its leadership. He took their calls and visited with them after Mass. He held regular joint meetings with the councils from both parishes so that the smaller parish felt it was part of the vision and the plan. He reported everything as it was decided and gave frequent updates to both congregations. He engaged the two parishes in developing a pastoral plan for the two communities—still separate, but collaborative. He contracted an outside, impartial facilitator to guide the process. Parishioners attribute the success of the linkage to his transparency and openness.

Pastoral Presence

Pastoral presence is critical in a linked situation. This means attention and care. Pastors need to be attentive and caring when they are with the faithful in each community.

Pastoral presence in multiple parishes must be intentional. With time so short, if it isn't intentional, it won't happen. Pastors may not be able to learn each person's name, but they can be attentive and present to everyone when they are together. An example of pastoral presence is greeting parishioners before or after a weekend Mass (doing both is rarely an option, because of Masses in multiple locations with little time between for travel). Pastors need to be accessible and careful to respond to calls from parishioners. A final example would be always mentioning first the parish where they are at the moment and never publically comparing the parishes.[47]

Pastoral presence does not mean attending every meeting or religious education gathering in every parish. Pastoral presence also does not mean that pastors should not delegate day-to-day responsibility to others. It simply means that while you are with a community or an individual parishioner, you are pastorally present to them in that situation.

Initially, pastoral presence will take the form of healer and comforter to the parishes experiencing loss and grief because of the linkage process. One pastor of two parishes realized early on that he needed to connect with his parishioners better and more often. He found that weekday Masses were a perfect opportunity because he wasn't rushing off to another parish. Each parish had three weekday Masses. He scheduled meetings and special events around those days when he had weekday Masses in each parish. He also did something fun with members of that community every week on one of those days—such as adult Bible study or coffee with the "God squad," the ten daily Mass attendees.

Another pastor relied on well-trained and effective pastoral ministers in two of his three parishes. He came when they wanted him. Otherwise, they were the pastoral presence in that parish on a day-to-day basis. But on weekends, when he came for the celebration of the Eucharist, he tried to always allow time before or after the Mass to greet and chat with people. He was careful to not schedule things that would truncate his time with that particular parish community.

In the end, pastoral presence is a matter of paying attention to the people being ministered to, not just to the ministry itself. It means good eye contact and good listening skills.

Collaboration

As mentioned in the previous chapter, the pastor must be collaborative and must facilitate collaborative visioning and decision making. As one pastor put it, "the mask and silver bullets have to go." The Gospel accounts of Jesus' instructions to the disciples, as well as the accounts of the early Church in the Acts of the Apostles and in the epistles, clearly establishes collaboration as the model of ministry. It is especially important for pastors of multiple parishes.

The work of the parish is not and should never be approached as solely the work of the pastor. John Paul II stressed that the parish is "the place where the 'mystery' of the Church is present and at work." [48] Because that mystery involves all the baptized, all the baptized need to be involved. Parishes are collaborative by their essence. The pastor who would be effective must cooperate with this essence and be a collaborator in the communities of disciples.

The majority of respondents (sixty-one percent) to the project survey on multiple-parish pastoring cited collaboration as an essential skill for which pastors needed training. Collaboration was among the three key pieces of advice pastors would give to others entering into this ministry. [49] The most obvious and necessary places where the pastor will exercise collaboration will be with the staff and parish lay leadership. We will deal with the staff more fully in the next chapter, so here we will focus on the collaboration with lay leadership.

The first instance of collaboration is the transition committee or task force that is formed by lay leadership from all parishes. This committee helps the incoming pastor gain an understanding of the culture and of the needs of the parishes. What makes each parish unique? What is important to know about the history of the parishes and their special customs, traditions, and significant events? The committee assists in a formulation of plans for the implementation of the linkage, which will be presented to the respective pastoral councils of the parishes. This plan would address initial staffing issues, interaction, and collaboration among the councils of the parishes; worship schedules including seasonal (Christmas, Triduum, Easter); breakdown of each parish's contribution to the salaries, benefits, and housing of the pastor; plans for the use of facilities; and measures to be taken to assist the parish members in transition. A complete listing of issues needing consideration during the linkage process can be found in the appendices.

Parish pastoral and finance councils constitute a second area of collaboration. Collaboration means wrestling with the issues. Issues facing the parishes need to be brought to the councils for consideration, prayerful discernment, and the appropriate responses. How will the parishes' identity as Eucharistic people be affected by the linkage and a cut in the number of Masses offered? How will the communities ensure that catechesis is available for members of all ages within the parishes? How will the resources be allocated? What needs to be done to grow the parish? Where will they find the volunteers to run the various ministries necessary for the life of the parish and well-being of the parishioners? These are just a few of the questions for consideration by the councils.

A primary responsibility of the councils is collaborative pastoral planning. We will deal with it in more depth later. Here, it is sufficient to simply mention it as one of the key areas in which a pastor will seek the collaboration of others.

As the linkage progresses, interparish councils and planning groups may be considered. Without these groups, pastors may find themselves doing too much "shuttle diplomacy." Bringing representatives from all the parishes together to collaborate on shared or cooperative ventures, programs, or systems allows the group to receive input from all parties. Each learns more about the other. Wonderful things can happen. They can be small things, such as the decision to publish a common bulletin; or more substantial projects, such as a joint stewardship program or the centralization of the catechetical programs.

Collaboration goes further than councils. Who needs to be involved in this discussion? Who needs to be asked for input on this issue? These are questions collaborative pastors ask. They are always cognizant of the fact that they are an important member of the community, but not the only member. At times, collaboration will involve the entire parish community. To do this, pastors call town hall meetings or use pew surveys. Some provide index cards and pencils in the pew and ask parishioners to respond to one question or suggested action. What you're looking for in this instance is the overall reaction to the issue at hand. Sometimes, this can lead to advice or suggestions for action.

Ultimately, collaboration brings others more fully into the mission. Lay leadership grows individually as they grow the Church.

Pastoral Planning

An effective pastor must be able to lead a community in visioning and planning for its future. This is especially true for pastors of multiple parishes. Said one pastor, "Let's face it. The only way we were able to get through that dismal place we found ourselves in at the first meeting of the four parishes was hoping that we were just passing through. We believed we were headed for better days, but we needed a vision and a plan to help us get there."

The pastor spearheads this effort of visioning and planning. The process involves visioning, assessing the current reality, and developing a plan to close the gap between the vision and the current reality. This visioning must be open to the guidance of the Holy Spirit.

In the visioning stage, the parish asks: Who are we called to be at this time and in this place? What are the values that must be protected and furthered? To what might God be calling these communities at this time, given their identity as disciples of Christ? There is also prayerful and careful listening to be done. How do pastors guide communities in determining their mission and vision? Where do they go to find direction and inspiration? We can suggest several sources.

- Scripture
- The teachings and tradition of the Church found in Vatican documents and statements from the USCCB
- Diocesan pastoral guidelines and letters

- Books and articles on the vision and theology
  of the parish
- The "best practices" of successful parishes and
  successful multiple-parish situations
- The histories, traditions, and experiences of the parishes

The visioning process leads to assessing current realities. The question is not about what needs to be fixed, so much as it is about identifying the gifts within the communities and seeing those moments when the Lord is at work. This stage requires looking for trends that would provide direction for the future. What might God be telling us? What might God be pushing us to consider? This is a time to be a people of hope, confident in the possibilities.

Next comes the development of a plan to realize the vision. The plan needs to be large and bold enough to challenge growth. The plan also has to be doable.

Pastoral planning will answer questions. Parishes will find their future through prayerful discernment of the guidance and gifting of the Holy Spirit. This is where you and your parishes discern the future for Parish A, Parish B, and Parish A and B together. Will we form one parish or remain two separate parishes? What areas of collaboration will help us reach our individual and common goals? What can we do together that has the potential for accomplishing more than what we could do individually?

Pastors need to be engaged in this process and in its implementation. By virtue of their office, they facilitate the process of articulating the vision and mobilizing the whole community. They help keep the vision "on the screen." They work with the councils and lay leadership to develop pastoral plans based on ideas that will bring the vision into reality.

Perhaps an example will help. The diocesan pastoral plan called for four parishes in the area to be linked. A transitional task force was formed with the pastor and representatives from each of the four parishes involved. They had a big problem. None of the four parishes had a worship site that was large enough to handle the crowds that would be coming to each mass. It was determined that they would need to consider a new worship site.

The inter-parish council began planning for a centrally located worship site. They suggested selling the four churches, investing that money into a gathering space and catechetical center in the central location, and then fundraising for the money to build the new church. They took the idea to the people who accepted it and supported it. They realized their vision with the participation of the members of all four parishes.

Conflict Management

Initial stages of linkages often involve conflict. Conflict management is an art that can be learned, and most pastors stress that if it isn't your skill, you should consider getting some training.

Managing emotions is paramount. Pastors should not take conflict personally, even if the expressions are presented in personal language. The issue usually isn't the leader; it's change itself. The leader will also want to set guidelines that insist upon civility and charity when discussing the issues.

Conflict can be resolved several ways: compromising, in which each party gives a little and gets a little; co-opting, in which one party wins the whole issue; or co-existing, in which each agrees to tolerate the other if it means they themselves won't need to change. The most desirable resolution is a solution that addresses all perspectives as much as possible. In business, this is referred to as "win/win." In multiple-parish conflicts, this is called simply "the pastoral solution."

Sometimes conflict involves differing expectations about the pastor. Expectations exist. A pastor can change them, but first he must identify them. (See Appendix D.)

One pastor of three parishes found himself criticized for not being present at the Sunday morning religious education programs, which were held simultaneously in all three parishes. "Father never goes to the classrooms. The kids never see him." The pastor recognized the conflict in its early stages. He knew it was based on unrealistic expectations that had carried over from the previous era, when there were pastors in each of the parishes. He asked that "Scheduling Catechetical Programming" be placed on the inter-parish council agenda.

When the time came, he told the council that he realized that the change had affected the tradition of the parish priest visiting the classrooms and participating in the programs. He also reminded everyone of the agreed upon Mass schedule that made his participation in the programming impossible. Then he posed the questions. "Should we change the time of the catechetical programs to an evening when I can participate? Should we change the Mass schedule so that I can participate in the programs at their current time? Should we combine the programs in one central location, so that I can interact with them before liturgy or so that they could be a part of the liturgy?"

The discussion that followed was spirited and productive. The council decided that centralizing the catechetical programs had merit. Each of the parishes had struggled to provide programming. They realized that the issue needed further study. So the group agreed that the programs would remain in their same time slot and that council members would work with the students and their parents, as well as with the volunteers, to explain the situation and the need for a change in expectations.

Conflict isn't always bad. Good things can flow from it. In this case, there was a cohesion that grew out of the collaborative consideration of the issues. The conflict also raised problems that hadn't been previously raised for consideration. The process encouraged the pastor and parish leadership to search for new ideas.

Community Building

The pastors who participated in the Multiple-Parish Pastoring Project emphasized the need for a new pastor to be a community builder: one who unified, who helped others to become people and communities of reconciliation, who healed the "brokenness," so as to form a whole.

The obvious challenge for pastors is to make a community out of different parishes. At times, this will involve skills in reconciling. At times it will involve healing. Those pastors who employ appropriate transition rituals often see themselves as more effective.[50]

The pastoral challenge of bringing together two parish communities is similar to the challenge faced by parents of a stepfamily or blended family. There is much that can be learned about working with multiple parishes from the studies on blended families, how they come together and yet remain separate. Among the guidelines often given to parents of a stepfamily, which could also apply to a pastor, include the following:

- Don't expect instant love between the two families (communities). It takes time for loving relationships to develop. Be patient.
- The new family needs to integrate some existing customs, rituals, and traditions, as well as create new ones.
- Each community brings to relationship different emotional, spiritual, and physical resources. Be aware that how you distribute these can create arguments, hurt feelings, or jealousies.
- Children (parishioners) have loyalties to their homes (parishes), parents, and pastors. Sharing a pastor initially may be difficult for parishioners to adjust to.
- Parents can't take all the responsibility for making this new family and this new relationship work. Children (parishioners) need to pitch in as well.
- Keep the number of a good family counselor (organizational consultant, trained diocesan staff person, or peer) handy—and call often.

Delegation

Pastors are responsible for the liturgical, catechetical, pastoral, and administrative aspects of the faith communities they lead. However, being responsible is not synonymous with personally doing the entire ministry. Delegation is a legitimate method for providing for the pastoral care and life within parishes. This is a point made by the USCCB document *Co-Workers in the Vineyard of the Lord,* which stresses not only the necessity of delegation but also its desirability.[51] Participants in the Multiple-Parish Pastoring Project also stressed its importance. Appropriate delegation sufficiently frees pastors to fulfill their essential roles and invites others to more fully live their baptismal calls.

Delegation requires clarity of parameters. What should the staff and parishioners handle on their own and what needs the approval of the pastor? Normal procedures need to be outlined. Job descriptions or ministerial covenants are in order. When something out of the ordinary develops, or when the individuals want to make significant changes to the normal procedures, approval from the pastor is needed. For example, a parish DRE would know that she needs the pastor's approval if she wants to join with a neighboring parish and hire an outside retreat director. This is out of the normal procedures as outlined and would need the pastor's support and approval.

One form of delegation that generated great interest among pastors was that of "multiplier ministries." These are pastoral workers who train other pastoral workers for a ministry. An example would be pastoral care for the ill and homebound. A pastor would recruit and train a core of people for this ministry. They, in turn, would recruit and train others. Together, pastor and volunteers would provide for the needs of the community.

One final comment: delegation needs to be done without abdicating pastoral responsibility. Pastors retain oversight over everything in the linked parishes.

Administration

We've never met a pastor who puts administration at the top of the "can't wait to do" list. We've also never met one who feels a calling to administration; they do it because it is part of their larger pastoral roles and responsibilities. Most will tell you they weren't trained for it and don't enjoy it. But the reality is, they are responsible.

"Get help!" is the advice from the symposium, the surveys, and the interviews throughout the project. Pastors are advised to find parish staff and volunteers who can handle the day-to-day administration of the parishes under their oversight. They further recommended that pastors get training wherever available through workshops, seminars, and courses offered by the diocese, seminaries and universities, and national ministerial organizations.

Parish administration has grown more complex. We will discuss personnel oversight and fiscal management separately. In this section, we will focus on the stewardship of resources, group and committee skills, and general administrative skills.

Stewardship is central to good parish administration. Being a good steward of the gifts and talents of the parish means that the pastor, staff, and parish leaders first have an "attitude of gratitude" with regard to the many blessings that are present in the parish communities. This includes the time, talent, and treasure of all. Secondly, it means that the pastor, working in close collaboration with staff, parish leaders, and parishoners at large, continually asks the question "Are we doing the best that we can to use the gifts entrusted to us responsibly, nurturing them respectfully, so that they will help the parish to continually grow in their ability to carry out the mission of Jesus?" This can only be accomplished through good parish administration, and the responsible management and distribution of all the gifts of the parishes.

The consultation and collaboration essential for effective pastoral leadership often takes place within councils and committees. Pastors and other participants in the project identified the following skills related to group work:

- The ability to clearly articulate a group's purpose within the context of the parish ministries and mission
- An understanding of the necessity of developing and following agendas at meetings
  - » An awareness of the dynamics of collaborative and consultative meetings
  - » Keep people involved
  - » Never use the time together to do what you could do alone (read minutes or reports)
  - » Always use the time together to do what you can't do alone—collaborate, brainstorm, collectively reflect, or problem solve
- The use of prayer to focus the meeting and facilitate discernment

General administrative skills identified in the Multiple-Parish Pastoring Project as necessary for effective pastors included simple actions, such as handling communication, returning phone calls, and scheduling appointments. They also included more complex approaches, like standardizing administrative programs and creating systems that would serve all the parishes. Additional administrative skills listed for their energy- and labor-saving benefit included the use of e-mail and conference calls rather than meetings that required travel between sites. Finally, a joint bulletin can help to coordinate the activities of the parishes and serve to form community.

Personnel Management

Project participants emphasized the importance of managing and leading personnel: the recruitment, hiring, training, supervision, and even termination of personnel.

Given the complexity and diversity of laws and diocesan guidelines, we recommend that when available, pastors stay in dialogue with the diocesan human resource office. These professionals can be of great assistance in successfully navigating these complicated issues before they reach a critical state. They will recommend such steps as performing background checks on all potential hires before offering positions or contracts.

Job descriptions or ministerial covenants are important for helping the staff understand the parameters and expectations of their ministry or service. Written personnel policies for the parish employees complement the job descriptions in establishing appropriate protocol and procedures.

Regular reviews were recommended to assist the pastor and the employee in determining how well expectations were being met, areas of accomplishment, and needed growth. Scheduled one-on-one meetings were necessary in supervisory relationships.

Fiscal Management

Fiscal management was strongly emphasized by project participants. While pastors rely upon consultation with finance councils, as called for in canon law, the fiscal responsibility still falls upon them. They need to clearly understand the budgeting process, which includes managing the finances of the parishes and raising funds.

Diocesan finance offices can help pastors understand relevant laws and required reporting. They often can provide advice about bookkeeping software for parishes.

Most pastors of multiple parishes do not handle the finances of the parishes directly. Most have staff or volunteers who input the figures, pay the bills, and oversee investments. But ultimately, the pastor is responsible for the fiscal health of the parishes served. Pastors and diocesan personnel all point out that most parishes have a great wealth of experience in financial matters within the congregation. Pastors are encouraged to find appropriate and trustworthy assistance from among the leadership to assist with these matters.

Clear financial accounting is especially important in the early stages of linking, where tension may arise about the finances of the separate parishes.

Time Management

One of the discoveries of age is that we will never "find time." The best we can hope to do is manage the time we have. One strategy often used by pastors is to realign expectations—their own and those of parishioners.

Pastors should look to their gifts when managing time. They should try to identify the aspects of their ministry that they find most life-giving and energizing, and then block out a chunk of time that will allow them to fully engage in that ministry. They should identify the aspects of their ministry that they find most draining and fatiguing and delegate those responsibilities to people with the necessary expertise.

Communication

Multiple-parish ministry requires communication. Effective pastors are good communicators. They recognize the importance of communicating information during the process so that everyone feels involved and engaged. They recognize that good communication also involves listening well and striving for mutual understanding.

Within multiple-parish ministry, it is virtually impossible to over-communicate. Instead the challenge is often finding the most effective means. Key vehicles include bulletins, parish newsletters, meetings of the parish councils and committees, meetings with staff and volunteers, meetings with interparish councils and task forces, announcements, bulletin boards, e-mails, and phone conversations.

It is especially important to communicate well through the transitional period of the linkage.

Stress Management

Stress occurs when expectations exceed the resources. Thus, stress in multiple-parish ministry is to be expected. Pastors can manage expectations using basic strategies: reduce the expectations, increase the resources available, and work smarter. The appendix includes a section dedicated to stress management.

Expectations for pastors come from several sources: self, staff, parish leadership, parishioners, and diocesan offices. A key strategy in managing stress is to reduce expectations to a manageable level. Delegation, communication, conflict management, and personnel oversight can be very helpful in dealing with unrealistic expectations and alleviating stress.

A second way of reducing the stress is to increase resources. The place to start is prayer, the energizing and nurturing time spent in relationship and dialogue with Christ. A second strategy involves looking to others to assist, delegating, hiring additional staff, recruiting key volunteers, and enlisting parish lay leaders to take a more active role in the provisions for parish life. A good stewardship program that promotes stewardship as a way of life marked by prayer, service, and generosity can turn a parish's resources of time, talent, and treasure from slim to abundant.

Finally, working smarter means maximizing the time one spends on those things that will have the greatest impact and will be the most effective and efficient, Likewise, it means minimizing the time spent on less productive measures that will have only a limited impact.

Ministerial Self-Care

One final skill for pastors of multiple parishes is ministerial self-care. Through healthy habits of self-care (spiritual, physical, intellectual, and relational), pastors increase their energy and effectiveness. Pastors participating in the project mentioned the need to

- Maintain a regular prayer regimen.
- Maintain a healthy regimen of diet and exercise.

- Schedule regular medical and dental check-ups.
- Take time away from the ministry weekly and take annual vacations.
- Stay in contact with family and friends.
- Continue formation through classes, seminars, or readings.
- Stay connected with peers in ministry.

What Have the Pastors of Multiple Parishes Shown Us?

We have learned that while the situation isn't ideal, it is possible to do well and to effectively lead multiple faith communities to growth. We have learned that the ministry can be life-giving. We have learned that pastoral effectiveness is often intentional. Effective leaders work on it and at it.

5

How to Recruit, Engage, and Empower the Pastoral Staff

MARK

When coaching pastors who are transitioning from single to multiple-parish pastoring, I often ask them to sketch out the schedule for a typical week. After they've done that, I tell them to cut the time in half. My point is that they will have only half the time for this parish. The rest of the time goes to the other parish. Pastors usually look at me with horror, saying this can't be done. My response is, "You have no choice."

I warn them that the pastoral needs and expectations in a two-parish situation will exceed the available time, energy, emotional, and spiritual resources. Then I ask, "How are you going to recruit, engage, empower, and support staff to meet the needs of the community?" Ideally the staff would be paid professional staff, but the staff is likely to include well-trained volunteers.

In multiple-parish situations, staff is critical. Failure to expand the pastoral resources by engaging others to assist is usually a ticket to burnout for the pastor. Without staff to assist, there is a real danger that the parish and pastor will sink into a survival mode of minimalism, making it a parish that has little chance of growth.

◇◇◇

KATE

The issues with pastoral staff are very complex. Staff provides a much-needed day-to-day pastoral presence for the faith communities, but they also require supervision and support. Staff members face challenges, as well. Those staff members in place at the time of linking are usually assigned additional duties. Maintaining the communication and interaction necessary for a healthy ministerial relationship with the pastor is complicated by the multiple sites within the parish.

Frequently, at the initial meetings for linking parishes, the lay leadership of the parish is reluctant to hire additional staff. "Father always did it by himself," I was told. To this I responded, "But that's not possible now, is it?" The issue all too often came down to money. I recommended that the money saved on the pastor's salary, considering the reduction in the number of priests, needed to be applied to auxiliary staff.

When I traveled about as the diocesan director of pastoral services, I was always impressed by the pastoral staffs who co-labored with the pastor. They were rarely specialists; most wore multiple hats. They usually ministered in more than one of the parishes that were linked. They provided an ongoing pastoral presence. They were the "go-to" people of the parishes on a day-to-day basis, the people who kept in close contact with the pastors. They usually were quite joyful people, knowing that their presence and their ministries mattered to the communities they served.

◇◇◇

What Do We Need to Understand about Pastoral Staff?

Co-Workers in the Vineyard of the Lord, the U.S. Catholic Bishops' document from 2005, stressed the need to include the laity in the ongoing mission of the Church.[52] The baptized are, by virtue of their baptism, commissioned to go out into the world as disciples engaged in the work of Christ as priest, prophet, and king. This participation is not based on a clergy shortage, but rather on their baptism. All lay Catholics are disciples gifted by the Holy Spirit.

Some will respond through occasional volunteer activity. Some will take on leadership roles, such as extraordinary ministers of the Eucharist, catechists, council members, committee members, and food pantry volunteers. But others will be lay ecclesial ministers, who have received training to collaborate more fully as co-workers of the pastor, in the provision of pastoral care for the faithful.

Many of them are "tapped" by a pastor or parish member who recognize their gifts.[53] Some take over existing positions. Some develop a new ministry to address a perceived need. Some discern their call on their own, receive formation for specific ministries, and respond to ministerial hiring processes.

Lay ecclesial ministers join with the pastor to form pastoral care teams that can more effectively and efficiently provide for the needs of the faithful and the demands of the mission. They minister in the areas of catechesis and evangelization, liturgy and spirituality, pastoral care and outreach, and administration of human and fiscal resources.[54] Without them serving as pastoral staff, the ministry of the pastor would "frequently be unable to obtain its full effect."[55]

How Critical Is Pastoral Staff to Multiple-Parish Ministries?

Pastoral staffs are crucial to the viability of modern pastoral situations. The expectations, hopes, and dreams for parishes are usually beyond the gifts and abilities of any one human being. Pastors participating in the Multiple-Parish Pastoring Project insisted that the parishes under their care will not thrive unless they are willing to engage, empower, and support pastoral staff. Furthermore, pastors risk burnout if they try to go it alone. Without staff, administrative duties can so monopolize their time that they are often unable to focus on the pastoral and life-giving aspects of their ministry.

Parish staff may be comprised of lay persons, members of religious communities, or permanent deacons. Deacons can provide additional assistance with preaching and with the sacramental ministries of baptism and marriage.

The majority (sixty-six percent) of parishes sharing a pastor have pastoral staffs. However, the majority of these are only part-time (eighty-five percent).[56] Parishes that share a pastor are more likely to share other staff than stand-alone parishes.[57] Pastors of multiple parishes identified pastoral ministers and business managers as being the most potentially helpful staff to have.[58]

It is important that the best people are chosen for staff positions. However, tensions arise when there is a desire to fill a position with a volunteer, rather than a paid employee. Volunteers are often chosen because they are available, not because they have the skills or ability to do the ministry. We recall a conversation with a pastor who was complaining about burnout. We asked him why he wasn't delegating more to the pastoral minister that had been prescribed as a necessary hire at the time of the linkage. He said that the finance council thought that a volunteer could do the job, so they recruited "Suzi" instead. Suzi was a wonderful woman, but as the pastor explained, "she isn't trained to do pastoral ministry. I can't delegate most pastoral ministry calls to her."

Staffing in multiple-parish models varies greatly from staffing in the "one parish, one pastor" model. Most (seventy-two percent) of the "one parish, one pastor" model parishes employ lay ecclesial ministers, while only a minority (forty-three percent) of parishes sharing a pastor employ lay ecclesial ministers. The ratio of pastoral staff to parishes is much smaller for parishes sharing a pastor than those of the "one parish, one pastor" model. In parishes that share a pastor, the ratio is .72 to a parish compared to 1.87 to a parish with its own pastor.[59] Put another way, parishes that do not share a pastor have two-and-a-half times as many staff people as parishes that share a pastor.

Linking parishes significantly impacts parish pastoral staff. At times, it leads to increased responsibilities for the existing staff as they take on additional tasks. At other times, new staff is added, changing the dynamics of ministry. Finally, the linking of parishes can lead to a realignment or reassignment of ministerial responsibilities for existing staff. [60]

What Are the Rewards for Parish Staff within Multiple-Parish Situations?

Parish pastoral staff that participated in the project spoke about the many rewards in serving in multiple-parish situations. The first was the creativity that flows from the synergy. New ideas, new approaches, new ways of doing ministry emerge. Pastoral staff members like the collaborative environment usually associated with linked parishes sharing a pastor. They find support from other ministers within the linkage and a willingness to share ideas, resources, and even work.

Another boon for the staff is an increased volunteer pool. New volunteers within the other parishes step forward to assist with projects and programs. Committees that had struggled in the past with few members get new life with new recruits from the larger pool. Overall, pastoral staff members find multiple-parish ministry to be satisfying, and even exciting, as they discover new possibilities when they begin to share a pastor with other parishes.

One director of religious education for a small parish described her enthusiasm for the new possibilities when her parish was linked with two others.

When we were entirely separate, things were difficult. Our numbers are small, but the hours spent coordinating and supervising the various aspects of the programs were the same as my peers serving in much larger parishes. The small numbers we had, at times, adversely affected the enthusiasm of the kids and adults that participated. Then, after we linked with the other two parishes, things began to change as we started to collaborate. We decided to do a joint summer Bible school for the kids. What excitement was generated! Following that success, we decided to try confirmation classes together. The teens loved it. There was just so much more energy in the program—and without any more work, because I was sharing the ministry with another director. In fact, at times, it was less work because we took turns with meetings and catechist trainings. It's working great!

What Are the Challenges for Parish Staff within Multiple-Parish Situations?

As one would imagine, the picture isn't entirely rosy. Some serious concerns and challenges arise within the multiple-parish ministry environment.

Probably the most common problem is tension that arises when the shared pastor has previously been pastor of one of the parishes in the linkage. There can be an initial stage of distrust and a question of loyalty between members of the combined staffs. One pastor in the project, Fr. Chuck, gave a good example. He had been the pastor of St. Ann's for eight years before it was linked with two additional nearby parishes. He noticed a tension whenever the staffs met, but couldn't put his finger on it until an argument erupted in a staff meeting over volunteer appreciation. "We know you're going to pick the idea of your staff over ours," said the liturgist from one of the other parishes. He added, "It makes sense. You know them better because you spent more time with them."

The mechanisms of multiple-parish ministry complicate the dynamics of pastoral staff teams. Pastors participating in the Multiple-Parish Pastoring Project identified five areas of concern that arose time and again: communication, stability in ministry, the pastor's skill and experience in collaboration, formation and training for staff, and supervision of staff. We will explore each more fully.

Communication

Establishing and maintaining good communication topped the list of challenges identified by pastors and staffs. They said that it is an issue that must be addressed early on. A key issue is contact with the pastor. Pastors must initiate and maintain good communication with staffs that are not always at the same site.

St. Aloysius, St. Bernard, and St. Mark Parishes all had separate staffs and their own resident pastor before they were linked. Most issues and questions were handled with a phone call, a chance meeting at the parish hall, a walk down the hall and a spontaneous conversation, or a short discussion after Mass. When the parishes were linked, all that changed.

The pastor was rarely down the hall. He had his offices at St. Mark's. He came to St. Aloysius and St. Bernard once a week, but the timing wasn't consistent. It often depended on his calendar and shifting pastoral care responsibilities. The short discussions after Mass were no longer an option because he always had to get on the road to make the next Mass.

The staff began to miss collaboration with the pastor. They felt separate, isolated, and sometimes even insignificant. The pastor, in turn, felt frustrated because he often didn't know what was going on in the various ministries at each of the parishes, and he was missing out on opportunities to connect with the staff and parishioners in meaningful ways. Things blew up when staff at each parish scheduled sacramental parent sessions at the same time and expected the pastor to be at all three.

The pastor consulted a fellow pastor of multiple parishes about leading staffs in these situations. The first piece of advice the mentor offered was, "Schedule separate and joint staff meetings." When the pastor said, "But my door is always open," the mentoring pastor stood firm. "Your time with staff needs to be intentional; it needs to be scheduled." A second piece of advice was equally important: "Set up a shared calendar."

Initially, the going was bumpy, but in time, it smoothed out. The staffs learned to think ahead and bring their issues or concerns to the monthly meeting. They likewise learned to enter their events and meetings on the shared calendar to avoid double booking, and to refer to the master calendar for the linked parishes in the initial stages of program planning. At first, they opted for separate staff meetings for each parish, with a joint staff meeting quarterly. After a year, they unanimously agreed that they liked the joint meeting better because it allowed for, and even encouraged, collaborative efforts across parish boundaries and creatively stimulated the staff members. The pastor felt that he benefited the most. He saved time. But more importantly, he saw that by working together, he and the staffs would grow the parishes in faith and mission. He no longer felt that he had to go it alone.

Regular, scheduled meetings with the staffs are imperative in multiple-parish situations. They facilitate communication not only between staff and pastor. Joint staff meetings encourage collaboration across parish lines. This usually translates into more vibrant parishes, and pastor and staffs that feel more focused and less fragmented in their ministries. Regular staff meetings allow the pastor and staffs to minister proactively and to work toward establishing a unifying vision that encourages collaboration. Regular meetings should be undertaken as soon as possible in the linkage process. If staffs already have a meeting pattern, then initially that should be honored. Over time, a new pattern for meetings can be determined jointly.

Good communication goes beyond staff meetings. Not everything can be anticipated ahead of time and brought to staff meetings. Challenges arise that established policies cannot handle. Staff members need to know how to contact the pastor, and the pastor needs to know how to reach the staff. This can be difficult when staff members work part-time hours.

If each parish has its own staff, clear channels of communication need to be established and honored. Phone calls and personal meetings aren't the only channels any longer. E-mail can be a great help in maintaining good communication between the staff members, the pastor, and a collaborative pastoral staff team. If the parishes don't have internet accessibility at their offices, adding it deserves consideration. Text messaging is even becoming an option for pastoral staffs trying to stay in contact with one another. The agreed upon channels should be employed. Equally important to the question of how to communicate is the assurance of both staff and pastor that their messages will be responded to in a timely manner.

Stability in Ministry

Stability of ministries is a second challenge raised by the pastors and staffs through the Multiple-Parish Pastoring Project. By stability, we mean two things. First, there is the stability of the ministerial positions following the change to a multiple-parish model. Second is the stability in ministerial responsibilities. Let's explore each more fully.

In any organization, when the leader changes, staff feels vulnerable. What is unique to the multiple-parish situation is the effect of change on parishioners. An already anxious parish community losing a resident pastor will not react well to the loss of staff as well. This is especially true if a parish's staff person is replaced by a staff person already working at the parish where the pastor resides.

Sometimes this instability arises because of varying styles of pastoral leadership. When Fr. Art accepted the pastoring of an additional parish, St. Timothy's, he was surprised by the number of part-time staff at the new parish. The previous pastor of St. Timothy's had wanted to engage as many people as possible in parish work. He hired twelve part-time employees to serve a parish of 1000 families. There were no full-time staff members. Fr. Art found the management of so many staff persons to be a logistical and administrative nightmare. But he recognized the need to move slowly. Over time he made some positions full-time and he identified staff members who could supervise others.

The tougher stability issue is that of ministerial responsibilities. The staffs are vulnerable to "job creep." Their responsibilities expand when the parish is linked with other parishes.

Some staff members that have responsibilities in one parish take on the same responsibilities at multiple sites. A director of faith formation for one parish suddenly becomes responsible for three smaller parishes that had no one doing this work. A director of worship and sacred music now has three choirs in three locations to coordinate and must plan liturgies for three separate communities, each using different liturgical aides and hymnals. A deacon assigned to one parish now must serve four, stretched across thirty miles.

The second kind of job creep is adding responsibilities to a job description because of the on-site absence of the pastor. An example would be the part-time pastoral minister whose original job description involved the visitation of the sick. After the linkage, this might also be doing sacramental preparation for the parish and handling the day-to-day administration.

Support staff members are especially susceptible to job creep because they are the only full-time staff in many of the smaller parishes. Their duties can increase enormously when there is no longer a resident pastor. They become the crisis manager, the keeper of the buildings and keys, the bulletin person, the bookkeeper, the calendar coordinator, and the day-to-day presence in the parish. They become the on-site pastoral minister by default, often having to do preliminary sacramental prep with individuals who want the sacraments, but are unaware of the policies or guidelines. Some support staff can handle these responsibilities and some can't. Pastors of multiple parishes need to be aware of these challenges. They especially need to guard against part-time staff being burdened with full-time responsibilities without adequate compensation or training.

In all of these instances, the issue at hand is one of justice. If a position is expanded, the job description should reflect the expansion. Pay for the expanded ministerial position should also reflect the changes in responsibility and duties. Some dioceses actually mandate that the money saved by reducing clergy salary and benefits be applied to new staff or to existing staff who will assume additional or new responsibilities.

What can pastors and staffs do to defuse the stability issue of expanded responsibility? Pastors and staff members participating in the Multiple-Parish Pastoring Project suggest the following. First, simply recognize that the dangers exist. Next, consider the needs of the communities sharing a pastor. How important is the stability of a pastoral presence of known and trusted staff to parishioners while the transition takes place? Is there a need for additional staffing? Can existing staff take on some more responsibilities without overtaxing them? What type of support do the staff members need in order to function properly, productively, and peacefully? Are the additional responsibilities that are passed on to the staff members just? Are the adjustments truly serving the parishes well?

The Pastor's Level of Skill and Experience in Collaboration

A third concern in the area of staffing a multiple-parish ministry is the pastor's skill in collaborative ministry. The importance of collaboration is a theme throughout every phase and component of the Multiple-Parish Pastoring Project. Pastors must be able to collaborate with others for many reasons: the mission is shared by all the baptized; the demands of the mission are too extensive for any one minister; the ministries within modern U.S. parish life have multiplied and grown more complex. For those leaders who are lacking skill or experience in this area, the dynamics of multiple-parish ministry operating at multiple sites only exacerbates the situation.[61]

A couple of problems in this area must be acknowledged. Not all pastors view collaboration positively. One pastor expressed his discomfort this way: "Collaboration is what the staff throw in my face when I make a decision without their input. That's crazy. I shouldn't have to consult on everything." A second problem area concerns pastors who subscribe to the "I do it best" model. They explain that it's hard for them to delegate or collaborate with others who aren't as experienced, knowledgeable, or talented. After all, they only want the best for the people. This may be true, but it also may be deadly, leading to burnout of the minister and offering the people less—because one person can't do it all.

What do we mean by collaboration? Perhaps the best and most applicable definition comes to us from Loughlan Sofield and Carroll Juliano in their book, *Collaboration: Uniting Our Gifts in Ministry.* They state that, "Collaboration is a style of performing ministry in a way that is completely based on the identification, release, and union of all the gifts in the Christian community so that the mission of Jesus Christ continues." [62]

Where does one learn this essential skill? Many dioceses annually offer continuing formation programs for clergy and laity. Often, these programs include sessions on collaboration and building staff teams. Diocesan offices of pastoral services may be a good place for neophyte pastors to connect in search of assistance, training, and support in collaboration. All of the national ministerial groups and organizations hold annual conferences, with workshops that specialize in the collaborative nature of modern ministry in the U.S. Finally, seasoned pastors can be tapped to serve as mentors to those just beginning who are in need of direction and support. Somehow, collaboration as a skill must be learned and practiced.

Formation and Training for Staff

Multiple-parish situations require staff. However, most parishes sharing a pastor are small and have little or no staff at the time they enter into the multiple-parish ministry model. Parishioners often step into the positions of staff out of a sense of service and dedication to their parishes, but they lack the necessary formation and training. Throughout the project, we frequently heard the concern that if the church is going to be grown, staff and volunteers must be given training and formation.

Training and formation of staff is especially crucial in multiple-parish situations because the supervisor often is off-site, unable to provide on the spot guidance and direction. Staff need to be able to function well without immediate assistance or constant supervision. Parishes need to provide for this training, they need to include the funding for it in the budgets, and they need to make sure staff members take advantage of training opportunities.

The career of a man we will call Fred illustrates the point. Fred had been using his experience in bookkeeping to serve as a volunteer administrative helper to the pastor. When the pastor retired, his parish was linked with another parish and shared a pastor. The new pastor was looking for someone who could help out on a more regular basis—paying the bills, drawing up reports for the councils and the diocese, and managing the weekly collection and deposit. Fred, who had retired from his job at the mill a few years earlier, volunteered to take on the additional duties. But his offer was contingent on getting training. He'd always done just what Fr. Jake had asked and exactly as Fr. Jake had instructed him. He didn't know much about the budget. The new pastor asked him to meet with an associate in the diocesan office of finance to learn about the diocesan system of accounts for parishes. He arranged for Fred to attend training for pastoral and finance council members, so that he better understood their financial report needs. Finally, with the support of the finance council, he provided the tuition for Fred to take two computer bookkeeping courses at a nearby community college. With the training and the support of the pastor and the parish lay leadership, Fred felt comfortable managing the day-to-day financial business of the parish.

Training for many staff positions can be gained through the diocesan offices affiliated with the specific position. Catechetical personnel can look to the Office of Catechesis or Religious Education for ongoing formation, training, and support. Most dioceses not only offer courses, but require certification for religious education/catechetical administrators. The Office of Finance can often provide training and support for parish bookkeepers. Ministerial associations within the dioceses frequently offer training and formation opportunities for those involved in catechetical, liturgical, pastoral, and administrative ministries.

College and university courses are another source of formation and training. Parishes often provide a portion of the tuition for degree training for newly recruited religious education administrators. Diocesan certification for ministry programs (institutes for lay formation) are also available in many places.

The solution needs to be arrived at collaboratively between the staff members, the pastor, and the parish lay leadership. The need for formation and training should be detailed in the job description and plans made to fulfill that need.

Supervision of Staff

Throughout the project, we learned of various ways that pastors were handling the supervision of staff. As with almost every aspect of multiple-parish ministry, there isn't one model. How staff is supervised, and by whom, needs to be worked out on the ground after surveying the situation.

Fr. Ted went from being the pastor of one parish to being pastor of three parishes. Two were larger parishes in small, neighboring cities. One was a small, rural parish. The larger parishes, with nearly 1000 families apiece, each had an elementary school with a principal, faculty, administrative staff, kitchen staff, a director of the catechetical programs, and a pastoral minister. One of the larger parishes had a director of worship and the other a director of sacred music. Both also employed full-time maintenance personnel and administrative support staff. The small rural parish had only one staff person—a part-time coordinator of religious education. Grounds at the smaller parish were taken care of by parish volunteers.

Fr. Ted individually met with the staff of each parish and discussed with them his quandary. As the pastor he had seventeen staff members to supervise, not including school faculty, administrative staff, and kitchen staff. This was too many for him to manage effectively. Therefore, he asked each principal to supervise all the faculty and auxiliary staff for their respective school. and he assigned one of the administrative staffers at each parish to supervise support staff and maintenance staff. Fr. Ted took responsibility for the supervision of the principal, catechetical leader, pastoral minister, director of sacred music, and auxiliary staff supervisor—eleven staff people in all. He arranged to have group staff meetings monthly. He set up a schedule of meetings with each staff person he supervised directly twice a year.

After one year, Fr. Ted realized that eleven people were too many to supervise well. The diocesan office of human resources recommended that he supervise from five to seven persons directly. He consulted with the staffs and the councils of the parishes about additional help with supervision. The more experienced and educated catechetical leader of the three parishes was asked to take the role of linkage catechetical director, supervising the other two. The director of liturgy was asked to assume responsibility for the coordination of all the liturgies in the linkage and to supervise the director of sacred music.

A linkage administrator was hired, who handled the supervision of the administrative staff and maintenance staff, and also assumed responsibility for the financial management in each of the three parishes. That left seven individuals for Fr. Ted to supervise directly. That, he felt, was more manageable for him and allowed for more personal supervision of all the staff.

Fr. Ted's example is out of the ordinary because of the size of the parishes he pastored. But we offer his example because it demonstrates the various options that are possible when seeking a solution to the question of staff supervision. The pastor does not need to be the supervisor for all the staff. In fact, in some cases we have seen pastors supervise only one person, the administrator who oversees everyone else. At other times, we have seen pastors assume the full responsibility for supervising staff. If the number of staff is small, this is feasible. However, when the number climbs above six, the quality of supervision begins to decline and the pastor will struggle with the weight of that large of a supervisory role.

What Else Has the Project Shown about Staff in Multiple-Parish Ministry?

There are four additional points from the project concerning staffs that are important to mention. The first is the need for all the staff sharing a pastor to also share a common vision.[63] Having joint staff meetings can assist with this common vision. A visioning experience or retreat early on in the process can also be beneficial. The earlier that vision is articulated, the better.

The second point is the need for staff members to share in the ownership of the multiple-parish situation.[64] Collaboration is vital. A team approach works well in generating participation and interest in the outcome.

The third point is the question of whether to maintain staff in each parish or to combine staff to work out of a common office. There are advantages and disadvantages to each model. When there is staff at each parish site, the parishioners often feel more cared for; with staff at the parish office, parishioners feel "they have a future." But separate staffs struggle with the distances and lack of accessibility to one another and to common resources. When the staff is combined at a common site, there is more day-to-day synergy. However, the parishes without on-site staff can feel less important, and even abandoned. The decision is one that needs to be made slowly, after much consultation, with the good of the whole cluster in mind.

The fourth and final point concerns paid versus volunteer staff. Volunteers must be engaged. Without volunteers, the work at hand simply cannot be accomplished. However, we believe that pastors of multiple parishes need at least one full-time staff person that they can count on day-to-day. Full-time staffers must be recruited, trained, and supervised, but they can assist immensely in the recruitment, training, support, and supervision of other volunteers.

Are There Any Final Words of Wisdom about Staff in Multiple-Parish Ministry?

Stay hopeful. Pastoring multiple parishes isn't easy, but it can be very rewarding for everyone involved. We've seen it work well in parishes across the U.S. We've seen tremendous growth in parishes that have pulled together and followed the lead of united pastoral staffs. Recognize the gifts given and shared. Spend time and effort supporting one another. This is the greatest praise offered to the Holy Spirit.

Models for Multiple-Parish Ministry

MARK

"The answer to your question is that we don't have an answer." Some of the most frequently asked questions in multiple-parish ministry don't have one right answer. The answer truly depends upon the situation, those involved, and the guidance of the Holy Spirit.

So what are the pastor, staffs, and parishioners supposed to do when they find themselves thrown together in inter-parish collaboration or multiple-parish situations? A number of basic models for organizing multiple-parish ministry have emerged. The first attempt to describe them was a monograph developed by Fr. Philip Murnion, the former director of the National Pastoral Life Center. Subsequently, I developed six models based on my experience in the Diocese of Green Bay. These models have come to be known as the "Mogilka Circles." Before getting into the models, however, we need to set the context.

Based on our experience, we have found that there is no single way to organize multiple-parish ministry. The best pastoral planning and decision-making processes involve collaborative decision-making that allows parishioners a voice, supports the pastor of the communities, and operates within the established policies of the local diocese and the universal Church.

Each model has advantages and disadvantages. While there can be some tangible advantages to multiple-parish models, we want to be very clear that in no way do we see these models as preferable to the traditional "one pastor, one parish" model.

While there appear to be six basic models, there are actually infinite variations of them. In fact, within a given cluster of several parishes, there may be different models that are served by the same pastor.

In the examples given, we portray a three-parish situation, but these basic models can be used for the linkage of two, four, five, or more parishes. The greater the number of parishes involved, the greater the challenge to the pastor.

Pastors and their communities may start a very simple model of inter-parish cooperation and collaboration, but they may progress to higher levels of inter-parish cooperation. A number of variables affect likelihood of inter-parish cooperation and collaboration.

◇◇◇

Does the Pastor Foresee Eventual Cooperation?

Pastors are advised to chart a basic course for the future of their parishes with regard to inter-parish cooperation. Does the pastor hope that the communities will grow closer together over time, or does he see that as unrealistic? A key question for pastors is whether the communities could merge in the long run or whether it would be better to keep them separate and more independent of one another. Probably the healthiest option is for the pastor to approach the task of serving multiple communities with an open mind and a desire to explore ways in which the communities can work together without a hidden agenda.

Our experience suggests that many communities can indeed grow so close that the lay parish leadership requests consolidation of the parishes. However, other parish communities that were linked ten to fifteen years ago have not grown in their ability to share programs, ministries, and resources. They still share the time and talent of the pastor and little else.

So what are some of the factors that increase and decrease the likelihood of inter-parish cooperation and collaboration?

Parish Cultures

Webster defines culture as "the sum total of ways of living built up by a group of human beings which is transmitted from one generation to another." Parishes have cultures. These cultures may make it more difficult for parishes to work together.

Parish cultures are not limited to ethnicity. One parish might see itself as a progressive parish, with the involvement of many lay leaders and a more liberal interpretation of church teaching and canon law. Another parish might see itself as more conservative in its approach to church teaching and liturgy. Increasingly, we are seeing parish cultures affected by a school. One parish is strongly committed to the support of a Catholic grade school. Another has invested more time and energy in parish faith-formation programs.

A pastor out West told us about the challenge he had trying to bring two small-town parish communities together. He couldn't understand why the two parishes just couldn't get along, cooperate, or collaborate with each other—until someone explained to him that even though the mines that once dominated the town have been gone for many years, historically St. Matthew's Parish was built and founded by the mine owners, while the second parish, St. Luke's, was built and founded by the mine workers. The animosity between the two went very deep, and was a difficult cultural barrier to work through.

Geography

In general, the greater the distance between parishes, the harder it is to facilitate growth in inter-parish cooperation and collaboration. We have also observed that while parishes may be in relatively close proximity to one another, things like high-ways, rivers, mountains, school districts, and shopping center preferences affect the ability of parishes to work together.

Leadership

What kind of leadership have the communities had over the past several years? To what extent has the bishop in the diocese or the parish leaders prepared parishioners to share a pastor with another parish? Has one or the other communities had the same pastor for many years prior to having to share a pastor? Have the lay leadership and parishioners been engaged in collaborative decision making? Do parishioners trust the pastor?

Relative Sizes of the Communities

It is easier to facilitate collaboration and cooperation between similar-sized communities. It is more difficult to get communities to work together when there is a size imbalance. In such situations, smaller parishes tend to be on guard and less cooperative, fearing that they will be gobbled up by the bigger parish. Larger parishes can view smaller parishes as a burden, and may resent the amount of time the pastor or staff spends serving them.

Demographics

What are the relative age profiles? Is one a younger parish, with lots of baptisms and children? Is one an aging parish, with fewer children and lots of funerals? What are the trends in the number of registered members, Mass attendance, schools, and faith-formation program enrollments? What does the census data for the area suggest in terms of projected growth—or lack of growth—for the area? What is the economic status of the neighborhood or small town? This information can usually be gathered from a local government planning commission, agency, or chamber of commerce.

All these factors influence inter-parish cooperation and collaboration. The pastors in these situations need to listen carefully to parish leadership as it feels its way along, maintaining a careful balance of respect for the roots of each parish, while continuing to explore ways that the communities can find win-win ways of working together.

The Models

Three basic variables need to be taken into consideration in the organization of multiple-parish ministry. Each can be placed on a cooperation continuum, from limited levels of cooperation to consolidated parish systems.

Pastors or Pastoral Leaders: At one end of the cooperation continuum you would have several parishes, each with its own pastor, trying to work together. At the middle of the continuum might be one pastor over two or more parishes who support a pastoral associate, deacon, or local staff person who acts as the day-to-day director of operations at the parish site. At the other end of the continuum you would have a pastor leading a single canonical parish that may have multiple worship sites, each with a few leaders with limited responsibilities.

The Staff and Programs: At one end of the continuum is a pastor who is responsible for two or more parallel staffs, each parish staff operating independently. The midpoint might be a situation in which various staffs meet periodically to coordinate calendars and do some inter-parish programming. They might even share some administrative staff, such as a bookkeeper or youth minister, or they might jointly support a school. At the far end of the continuum you would find one pastor who leads one staff, who probably have all their offices at one site and together serve the various parishes, churches, or facilities that are part of the linkage of parishes.

Parish and Inter-parish Councils: At the beginning stages of facilitating inter-parish cooperation and collaboration, each parish in the linkage would have its own pastoral and finance council operating independently of one another. There may be an inter-parish coordinating committee that meets periodically to share information and to consider ways in which the parishes can work together. At the midpoint of this continuum, instead of being just a "coordinating committee," the inter-parish council becomes more of an area pastoral council. Also at this midpoint, there is probably an inter-parish budget that pays the salary for the pastor, some staff, and some shared programs. While each parish still maintains separate pastoral and finance councils, the pastor of the linkage increasingly relies on the advice of the area pastoral council to do what's best for the entire Catholic community in the area. At the far end of the council continuum, there is one area pastoral and one area finance council. The gifts and resources of the respective communities have been consolidated.

Model I—Separate Parishes—Coordinated

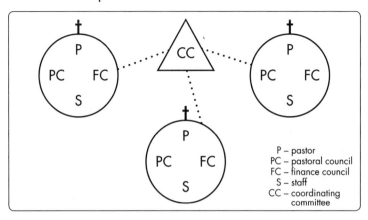

P – pastor
PC – pastoral council
FC – finance council
S – staff
CC – coordinating
committee

Each circle in the diagram for Model I represents a separate, independent parish. Each parish has a pastor (P), a pastoral council (PC), and a finance council (FC). Each parish also has its own staff (S). At the center of these linked parishes is a small triangle that represents a coordinating committee (CC).

This model is typically the first model used to try to facilitate inter-parish cooperation and collaboration. Sometimes, it is tried by pastors who believe in the value and potential benefits that can be achieved when parishes in a geographic area cooperate and share their gifts and talents with one another. Other times, this model has been presented as part of a diocesan pastoral planning process in which linked parishes will need to learn to work together, with a goal of eventually transitioning to a shared pastor model.

This model has been referred to as "the polite model." It works as long as everyone who comes to the coordinating committee (CC) meeting is polite, respectful of one another, and committed to seeking ways to share resources and identify win-win solutions that will equally enhance each parish.

Some Advantages of Model I

- This model is widely used throughout the country. A number of dioceses have reorganized all their parishes into linkages that are similar to Model I. It is a good place to start to build trust and relationships, and to explore possibilities for inter-parish cooperation and collaboration.

- Parishes that are brought together using Model I know that, in time, one or more of them will be sharing a pastor with another parish. If there is a marriage in your future (the sharing of a single pastor between parishes), then it is a good idea to begin dating now! Model I is a great way to start dating before the direct linking, or marriage, of parishes under a shared pastor.

Some Disadvantages of Model I

- This model often lacks clarity about the mission or purpose of the coordinating committee (CC).

- Members are more concerned about what's best for "my parish" then about what might be best for the good of their Catholic community.

- It is often difficult to get separate parishes to come to consensus on decisions when everyone around the table is an equal and there is no leadership authority structure. Because consensus is used, individuals or members from one parish may block consensus efforts that might be supported by a majority.

- Using collaborative decision-making processes, significant proposed actions by the coordinating committee (CC) can rarely be acted upon in a timely manner. This is usually because they need to be reviewed by the pastoral and finance councils in each of the respective parishes before coming back to the coordinating committee (CC) for a decision.

Model II—Separate Parishes—One Pastor and Local Leadership

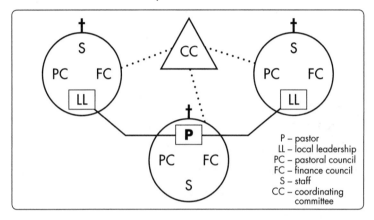

P – pastor
LL – local leadership
PC – pastoral council
FC – finance council
S – staff
CC – coordinating committee

In Model II there is only one pastor (P), who is the pastor for each of the parishes in the linkage of three parishes. Typically, the pastor in this model resides in one of the parishes where he provides leadership, ministry, and oversees the day-to-day operation of that parish. In each of the other two parishes, significant local leadership (LL) is empowered and supervised by the pastor (P) to provide leadership and ministry and oversee the day-to-day operation of each parish. While the pastor (P) is the canonical pastor for all three parishes, local leadership (LL) takes care of the parishes in many if not most areas except for sacramental ministry. The sacramental ministry may be provided by the canonical pastor or by a retired or neighboring priest who resides in the area.

In the ideal form of Model II, the local leadership (LL) is a full-time, paid, well-trained, and well-formed pastoral associate—a lay person, religious, or deacon—with a master's degree in pastoral ministry or theology and several years of full-time experience in pastoral ministry, faith formation, or parish administration. Often, such leaders are able to provide ministry in most areas of parish life—with the exception of sacramental ministry. Pastors of such individuals are able to delegate significant amounts of responsibility, and these people only need limited supervision and oversight.

However, the ideal for Model II is not always realized. The research by Sr. Katarina Schuth—and our own experience—indicate that most parishes that share a pastor lack such well-prepared staff. In the vast majority of multiple-parish pastor situations, there may be staff with minimal training and experience or no staff at all.

In parishes with no paid staff, local leadership (LL) is often made of volunteers from the parish community, who take care of the day-to-day operation of the parish. Ideally, these volunteer parishioners will have received some training and formation, in areas such as pastoral care, education, youth ministry, liturgy, parish business administration through diocesan lay ministry formation programs, or through mentoring in these roles from the pastor. Local leadership (LL) should also include well-organized parish pastoral and finance councils. Pastors without paid staff often have to spend considerable time being present to, supervising, and monitoring the local leadership (LL)

There are many possibilities between the ideal of well-trained, full-time paid staff on the one hand and all-volunteer local leaders (LL) on the other. Because parishes that share a pastor tend to be small, the most common situation is one in which the local leadership (LL) initially takes the form of a full- or part-time secretary. Secretaries, usually women, provide often-unrecognized—and yet, at times outstanding—ministry in the forms of day-to-day parish administration, pastoral care, and education in the faith. In the absence of the pastor, they may be the face of the parish, the person who cares for parishioners and those who are in need from the broader community.

Another approach to providing leadership in parishes where a pastor does not reside is through the appointment by the bishop of what is most commonly called Parish Life Coordinators (PLC). By 2008, bishops had appointed 477 lay, religious, and deacons, and delegated to them the responsibility for the pastoral care of parishes as allowed under Canon 517.2. In several dioceses, parish life coordinators have also been appointed by the bishop to serve two or more parishes as on-site "pastors." For the most part, they serve their communities very well.

When a bishop appoints a PLC to a parish, the responsibility for providing the pastoral care of the parish now shifts from the pastor to the PLC. The result is that the original pastor no longer has responsibility for the parish and is technically no longer in the multiple-pastoring situation. In our experience, it is not uncommon for pastors of multiple-parish situations to hire well-trained and well-formed local leadership (LL), mentor them, and then act as advocates in the presentation of these leaders to the bishop for appointment as parish life coordinators in accord with Canon 517.2.

There are still other situations we are aware of, where a pastor will hire well-trained and formed local leadership (LL) and tell them, "Between you and me, you are acting as a parish life coordinator—you run the parish. I'll be there for you and provide sacramental ministry, but it's your parish." There are many problems with this approach: namely, the lack of authority from the bishop that the local leadership should be accorded, lack of diocesan training and formation available to pastors and parish life coordinators, and lack of access to local and diocesan meetings of pastors and parish life coordinators. Yet this practice is much more prevalent than most will acknowledge. We understand that in some dioceses this is necessary. We only wish more local leaders could be acknowledged, affirmed, and appointed by bishops in accord with Canon 517.2.

Those interested in learning more about this should read the book *Parish Life Coordinators: Profile of an Emerging Ministry* (Loyola Press). It presents the findings of the Emerging Models of Pastoral Leadership Project on Canon 517.2 leadership. Also check the Web sites for the Emerging Models of Pastoral Leadership Project and CARA.

Some Advantages of Model II

- Many of the day-to-day administrative and pastoral responsibilities of running a parish can be delegated, thereby relieving some of the burden on the pastor.
- There is someone on-site who can handle many of the day-to-day needs of the parish and can represent the pastor in key matters when he cannot be immediately present.
- Some pastors in multiple-parish situations find that they no longer have time to develop any relationships

with parishioners, because their administrative responsibilities are so extensive. By delegating responsibility to someone on-site in each of the communities, the pastor can once again be more pastorally present to parishioners in at least one of the parishes for which he is responsible.

- Communities that are concerned about their future viability and maintaining their identity take comfort in knowing that they still have their own staff, own pastoral and finance councils, and own unique programs and ministries.

Some Disadvantages of Model II

- It is sometimes hard for a community to accept the leadership and pastoral care of someone other than a priest. Catholics are accustomed to the idea that parishes are led by priests. When that is not possible, a period of readjustment and reorientation is needed. However, our experience suggests that most communities are able to overcome their reservations and find the local leadership (LL) to be very good for all concerned.
- Often, the perception arises that the favored parish is the one where the pastor resides. As a result, there can be jealousies between the parishes.
- In Model II, there is often a coordinating committee (CC). As in Model I, it takes a great deal of effort to reach real cooperation and collaboration between parishes.
- Sacramental ministry in Model II may not be provided by the canonical pastor. In those situations where the

canonical pastor is not the sacramental minister, it is important for the sacramental minister and the pastor to work together so that the minister is well-briefed on the background of the person or family who is coming to the sacraments. This is especially important for baptisms, weddings, and funerals, and in those situations where the pastor knows the families well and has spent hours with the parishioners in preparation for reception of the sacraments.

Model III—Separate Parishes—One Pastor

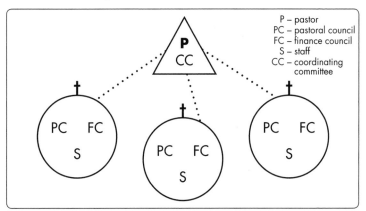

The key characteristic of Model III is that there is only one pastor (P) who provides leadership and pastoral and sacramental care for each of the parishes. The pastor is the "go-to guy" for each of the parishes. There is no designated local leadership as in Model II. Each parish maintains a separate pastoral council (PC) and finance council (FC). The parishes may have some limited staff (S).

Because there is only one pastor, the role of the coordinating committee (CC) is stronger than in previous models. In this model there may be the initial development of an inter-parish budget, with each of the parishes at least sharing costs for the salary and living expenses of the pastor and perhaps even, on a limited basis, some inter-parish programs and ministries.

In this model there is a tendency for the pastor to take the advice and wisdom of the coordinating committee (CC) more often than that of the individual pastoral councils (PC) and finance councils (FC). The really good pastors still try to work to achieve a consensus among and between the parishes. When necessary, the pastor can choose to not follow the advice of one or more of the individual councils if the recommendations of the minority councils are not seen as in the best interests of the whole linkage.

Based on research on parish reorganizations done by the Conference for Pastoral Planning and Council Development, this model is the least preferred by pastors, since it demands the most from them as they try to serve two or more communities and maintain multiple parish organizations equally. With Model III, it is very difficult for pastors to live up to the demands and expectations of multiple-parish communities. (See Appendix A for "Pastor and Parish Job Description.") It is very difficult for pastors to support and maintain multiple, unique parishes with separate pastoral and finance councils, staffs, facilities, traditions, and budgets.

Conversely, it should be noted that this is the model that parishioners and lay leaders in the parishes most often prefer if they have to share a pastor. The lay leadership still feels like they have some control of their boundaries, identities, future, and budgets through the actions of their independent pastoral and finance councils and through a staff who serves and advocates for their needs.

Some Advantages of Model III

- The pastor has the authority to make decisions for the good of the linkage and the individual parishes.
- Parishioners feel they still have some control over their parish business and activities with individual parish pastoral and finance councils.

Some Disadvantages of Model III

- Pastors still need to do "shuttle diplomacy."
- Pastors struggle with the "meeting explosion" arising from so many councils.

Model IV—One Pastor—Centralized Team and Council

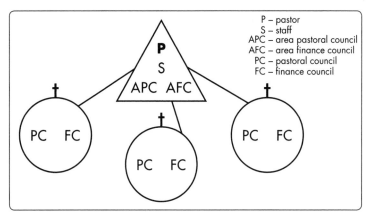

The key change in Model IV, as compared to the previous model, is that the staffs of all the parishes are combined into one. In most instances, the combined staffs form a team that has their offices in the same location. Together they serve the parish communities at each of the churches that are part of the linkage.

In this model there is a significant shift of responsibility and influence from the individual pastoral councils (PC) and finance councils (FC) to greater reliance on the work of the area pastoral council (APC) and the area finance council (AFC). Because there is one staff in this model, and most programs and services are coordinated by this common staff in service to the parishes, decisions and plans for the future of all are developed in and through these central bodies.

Some Advantages of Model IV

- This is the model preferred by most pastors, because now they have one staff working out of one site, which makes it easier to supervise. The pastor's ability to be present to staff facilitates greater staff cooperation, collaboration, and decision making.

- The common staff makes it easier to share the gifts, programs, and ministries between the various parishes. The result is a decrease in the level of administrative wear and tear on the pastor.

Some Disadvantages of Model IV

- Parish lay leaders are often reluctant to consolidate many of the staff and programs, especially if that would mean that the local parish offices would close. They are concerned that this move would require travel to the joint or inter-parish office that may not be as convenient.

- Parishioners fear losing their parish identity: "Everything will become standardized" or "We'll have to do Mass the way they do it over there, not the way we do it."

- Parishes think that if they cooperate too much, it will be easier for the new pastor or the diocese to close their parish in the future.
- Individual parish pastoral councils (PC) and finance councils (FC) lose some of their power and influence. Most core ministries, programs, and budgets are managed out of the central office. The individual parish councils may still organize some activities unique to the specific local parish community and continue to insure the maintenance of facilities, but even these activities are subservient to the action of the central office and leadership team.
- Even when utilizing Model IV, it is necessary to provide staff, support, and guidance to separate pastoral councils and finance councils

Model V—Merged Parish

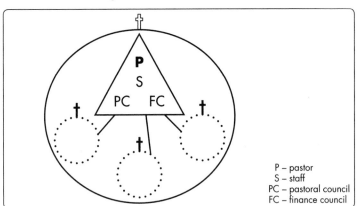

P – pastor
S – staff
PC – pastoral council
FC – finance council

In Model V there is a consolidation not just of the staff, but of the pastoral councils, finance councils, and assets and liabilities of each of the parishes. Canonically, one new parish is created. Instead of multiple-parish consultative structures there is just one, and it has responsibility for working with the pastor and staff to serve the entire Catholic community in the area. At least initially, the community will probably continue to worship at multiple worship sites.

Some Advantages of Model V

- There is only one set of councils: one pastoral council (PC) and finance council (FC).
- This structure allows for the community to maintain multiple churches/worship sites.
- It is easier to standardize committees, policies, and procedures across community sites.
- There is usually only one staff at a common, central location.
- It is easier to make decisions regarding the best use of building and facilities on the basis of their support to the joint mission.

Some Disadvantages of Model V

- The original parish communities may experience anxiety and fear about the loss of their identity and control over the programs, staff, and finances.
- If one of the parishes was in debt prior to the merging of the parishes, there can be resentment by the debt-free congregations that their hard saved assets will be used to pay off the debt of the "irresponsible" parish.

- There is concern about who will care for the cemeteries at each of the original parishes.
- There is a fear that the "one big parish" will be less personal than the former, smaller "family parishes."

Model VI—Build and Close

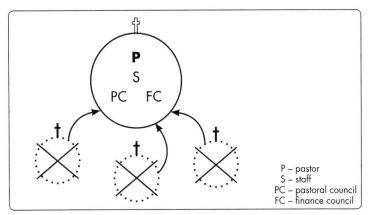

P – pastor
S – staff
PC – pastoral council
FC – finance council

This is the most radical of the models. The original worship sites are closed and a new, common worship site is built. This may be done because old buildings are deteriorating. Or it may be driven by the realization that none of the former individual worship sites is adequate to hold all who want to attend Mass on Sunday mornings for major feasts. The leadership comes to the awareness that they need to build a single worship site, which can partially be paid for through the sale of previously used sites

Some Advantages of Model VI

- There is a sense of pride, accomplishment, engagement, and ownership that comes when a community builds a new church.

- There is a deep and profound satisfaction that comes from building something that will serve the Catholic community for years to come, a place for the community to worship God for generations to come.
- There are savings in the long run, because of the energy efficiency of newer buildings. With the sale of the original buildings and campuses, there are savings realized in maintenance and in travel.
- There is less wear and tear on the pastor and staff because they no longer have to travel to multiple sites.

Some Disadvantages of Model VI

- There is a loss of the smaller family parishes and the intimacy of those communities.
- There is pain and grieving that accompanies the closing and sale of worship sites/churches.
- There is often a loss of parishioners who are upset by the closing of the original churches.
- There is usually a debt incurred when the new site is constructed.

Concluding Thoughts

There truly is not one answer that fits all situations. These models provide a beginning, a way that we have seen parishes move forward in collaboration and cooperation. The models may evolve over time. The final model is not the best model, "to be achieved no matter what." It is only another model that, at certain times and in specific places, makes the most sense from the perspectives of discipleship and stewardship. What is important is not a methodical march to the next model, but an intentional evolution to greater cooperation and collaboration for the good of all. The progress will depend largely upon the compatibility of communities, based on such variables as demographics, economics, culture, and leadership.

7

If It's Working,
What Does It Look Like?

MARK

The criteria for successful multiple-parish pastoring that are listed in this chapter come from the experience of pastors and staff who have moved into multiple-parish situations.

Multiple-parish ministry is about making the best of a less-than-ideal situation. Like it or not, these are the gifts and resources with which we have to work. How are we going to be good stewards of this situation in a way that will help further the mission?

It is critical, as you make the transition from single to multiple parishes, to recognize that there is a period of disorganization, resistance, grieving the past, and anxiety about an unknown future. The role of the pastor is to guide, accompany, and love the people through the wilderness. A successful transition doesn't happen overnight. It takes time and loving and compassionate leadership. It takes at least eighteen to twenty-four months for the communities to emerge on the other side.

◇◇◇

KATE

When I first began working with multiple-parish ministries as a Director of Pastoral Services, there wasn't much enthusiasm for assigning pastors to multiple parishes. It was regarded as necessary, not desirable. I was amazed at the low expectations. The response "We'll manage" got my goat. Nowhere in Scripture can I find Christ telling the apostles to settle for "managing." No, Christ was all about growing the kingdom, not maintaining the status quo or settling for what is manageable.

But then, multiple-parish pastoring took off. Certain pastors assigned to multiple parishes were thriving. Their parishes swarmed with enthusiasm. Their membership took on responsibilities. They didn't play dirges at the liturgies; instead, they gathered together and celebrated their new sense of community and participation in the mystery that was their faith.

Multiple-parish ministry is not the ideal, but it is possible to grow the church and the faith of the individuals in multiple-parish situations. Those who succeed share several traits. They offer a template of what is possible. The Multiple Parish Pastoring Project validated the observations I had made through my years of working with multiple-parish ministries as a diocesan director and through my research for my doctorate project and thesis.

⬦⬦⬦

How Did the Multiple Parish Pastoring Project Identify the Traits of Healthy Linkages?

The information about healthy linkages came from a number of project resources. These include a phone survey of diocesan leaders, phone interviews with effective pastors of multiple parishes, and symposia that gathered the insights of pastors, parish staff members, and diocesan staff members. In time, we came to see that the healthy linkages shared many traits with the healthy and vibrant parish, as identified in earlier research by the Notre Dame Study of Parish Life, the Parish Project by the National Pastoral Life Center, and the national survey on pastoral excellence sponsored by Emerging Models of Pastoral Leadership Project.[65]

When it came time to present the training program for multiple-parish ministry as part of the project, Mark Mogilka and the committee summarized the data in a list of six traits for a healthy linkage. We will explain them individually.

- Unity flowing from common goals and priorities
- Stability achieved through successful transitioning
- Stewardship as a governing principle

- Growth of the parishes
- Balance between the needs of the individual and those of the linkage
- Life-giving ministry from energized ministers

Unity Flowing from Common Goals and Priorities

Collaboration, the essential dynamic in multiple-parish ministries, needs common goals and priorities. Without them, the individual parishes compete, rather than collaborate. These building blocks of collaboration require intentional group work on the part of the pastor, staff members, and parishioners of all affected parishes.

A common goal that is often not articulated is that each of the parishes involved wishes to survive as a parish. It isn't articulated because, at first blush, it sounds self-serving. But it isn't self-serving, because a parish's desire to survive is basically a desire to find the appropriate manner in which to celebrate and grow its faith and reach out to others. Through the guidance of the Holy Spirit, parishes may eventually see that their survival requires their joining together more closely, perhaps even to merge into one parish. In other words, occasionally the only way to ensure that the faith of the community will survive is to give up the life it has known for a different life. It is the paschal mystery lived out on a community level.

Still, the desire to survive is strong at the initial stages of a linkage. Each of the parishes sharing a pastor needs to benefit from the relationship if the endeavor is to succeed. Establishing common goals and priorities is a way to do this. Common goals should be a priority from the beginning. A common mission statement for the linked parishes can help unify the separate communities and staffs. A common mission statement certainly helps the pastor, who can rely upon it for guidance and who draws from it a cohesiveness that enhances his ministry. Developing the common mission statement is one of the most important tasks of the leaders from all the parishes involved as they join together to plan for their future.

The common mission statement is especially important for the pastoral staffs. Even if the staffs are not meeting jointly on a regular basis, they need to develop an overarching mission statement that steers them clear of competition and leads toward collaboration.

This situation is in many ways similar to an interdenominational marriage. Historically, the emphasis was on differences between the two. Yet in recent years, emphasis has shifted to the many points of agreement between Christians of different denominations. These common beliefs are the basis for a strong bond. Similarly, in multiple-parish situations, it is helpful for parishes to emphasize the traditions, beliefs, and values they hold in common, rather than dwelling on their differences.

Once the common mission statement is developed, the parishes need to identify two to three priorities that they will work on collaboratively during the coming year. This list of priorities needs to be updated every year that the parishes share a pastor.

Many times in the Multiple Parish Pastoring Project, we heard about parishes that had been concerned about losing services finding ways to retain them through collaboration and the support of the other parishes in the area.

Stability Achieved through Successful Transitioning

A healthy linkage depends on successful transitioning. The goals of the initial stages of the process are to replace uncertainty with stability, competition with collaboration. Initially, people will resist change. Some will find the loss of a particular Mass, a certain program, a long-standing tradition more than they can accept. But if the transition is handled well, these individuals will usually remain a minority.

Within the Multiple Parish Pastoring Project, we repeatedly heard that the leadership must steer the parish membership away from simple survival mentality and toward a desire for growth. This requires hope. A common mission statement and established priorities provide a foundation for that hope by demonstrating that each parish is integral to the whole. Hope is to be found in the possibilities that weren't always available when each parish stood separately. In successful transitions, anxiety arising from the uncertainty of what is to become of the individual parishes eventually gives way to confidence in a future for the faith communities.

A second step in transitioning is moving to shared multiple-parish ministries. It begins with the pastor, but it also includes sharing youth ministry, pastoral care, catechetical programming, or administration. The benefit of multiple-parish situations is demonstrated when services that individual parishes were not able to support are undertaken collaboratively.

Marriage is a good analogy for a healthy linkage. Christian marriage expands the "me" and "you" to include an "us." This is also true of parish linkages. The goal is to find ways to get away from the limiting and polarizing "me" versus "you" to a healthier attitude that includes "we." We are not advocating the loss of "my parish." We anticipate that people need to still talk about "my parish" and "your parish." But we want to encourage them to also talk about and celebrate what happens when "we" work together.

Pastors repeatedly said that talking openly about the needs and concerns of each parish contributed to the transitioning into a collaborative linkage. This follows the example of St. Paul who often brought the needs of one faith community to another in an effort to build up the body of Christ.

Stewardship as a Governing Principle

Some of the biggest obstacles to achieving a successful transition to the multiple-parish pastoring model are the multiplication of Masses, meetings, miles, and ministries. Those who overcome these obstacles usually point to the practice of stewardship. The multiple-parish situation clearly illuminates the need for everyone to get involved in the mission. There is simply too much to do. There is no room for spectator spirituality and disengaged disciples. Everyone is called upon to share their time, their talent, and their treasure.

Stewardship not only requires a sharing of what has been received; it also requires an awareness of the blessings. Stewardship embraces the abundance that flows from God. Each parish and each individual within the parishes have been gifted and blessed. Stewardship helps us realize that we have been entrusted with the responsibility of caring for and utilizing these gifts and blessings. The key stewardship question is, "How can we make the best use of these gifts for the sake of Christ's mission?"

Stewardship requires managing what we have been given. Healthy linkages use all the resources at hand—human and material. One way of doing this is to consolidate duplicate services. Examples include going from separate bulletins for each parish to a shared bulletin, joint sacramental preparation programs for marriage and baptism, and joint reconciliation services during Lent and Advent. Human resources are respected when leaders, staff, and parishioners practice subsidiarity, the principle that matters be handled at the lowest, most appropriate level. Subsidiarity in action could be parish members taking responsibility for unlocking the church and setting up for weekend liturgy or parish staff registering new members. Parish leaders and parishioners alike ask themselves who can and should do something.

Not just the management, *but the stewardship* of the material resources is equally important. What is the best use of buildings? How will the rectories be used? Can they be adapted into office spaces for needed staff? Do they need repairs or updating in order to make them more useful? What about the financial resources of the parishes? Are they being managed well? Does each parish have an annual budget and a long range maintenance budget? Are the monies saved in pastoral salary and benefits being reinvested in needed staff? Does it make sense to centralize the administration in order to save on travel time and the expense of multiple offices? Are we being good stewards of our material blessings by maintaining and heating two churches, when combined communities could easily worship at one or the other?

Growth of the Parishes

Initially, parishes may focus on survival. Those who succeed look past survival, to the more important issue of growth. The question is not whether the parish can survive, but how it will thrive. Many multiple-parish linkages grow in membership, Mass attendance, community participation, catechetical program enrollment, and finances.

We grow through evangelization. We also grow in our personal faith through the witness of others, through moving and meaningful liturgies and celebrations, and through ongoing, lifelong faith formation.

Balance between the Needs of the Individual Parishes and Those of the Linkage

Parish linkages need to balance the needs of the parishes and the needs of the linkage as a whole. Marriage provides a good analogy. Strong marriages are characterized by a balance between "I" and "we." Husband and wife honor their uniqueness, while working together for a shared vision and life. The same is true in successful parish linkages.

Within linkages that succeed, the roots, traditions, and history of each parish are affirmed and respected. Yet the parishes are able to come together to work for the common good of all. The antithesis of this is the linkage where one parish dominates and the others acquiesce to keep the peace.

Life-Giving Ministry from Energized Ministers

Linkages that succeed are led by energized ministers who find their ministry life-giving. Expectations are important. They must be realistic for the minister, for staff and key lay leadership, and for the parishioners. The workload must remain manageable, with time off for renewal and rest. Healthy linkages are led by pastors who take on the aspects of their ministry that they do most effectively and delegate the rest to persons more suited to handle them. Pastors who are thriving recognize their own limitations and take care of themselves. This means annual retreats, ongoing formation, good and healthy life choices, practices including "days away," and an active prayer life that leads them to a holistic approach to ministry. Their spirituality, intellect, and ministerial experiences must connect and illuminate each other.

Seek the Best for the Most

Linkages that succeed share a common mission and priorities. The parishes involved work together for the good of one another. They transition well because they recognize the challenges of change and work together to ensure the growth and enhancement of each member. They see the challenges realistically, yet can see beyond them to a future that they believe is possible. They practice good stewardship of both human and material resources, calling everyone into action and using each gift and resource responsibly. They don't just get by. They are not satisfied with surviving. They seek to thrive. They make concerted efforts to grow the local church by increasing membership, Mass attendance, and community participation. The congregations go from membership mode to discipleship mode, calling everyone into active participation and providing catechesis to help them understand and live their faith more fully.

If linkages are to succeed, the members must participate in the communal paschal mystery. There is a dying involved, but there is also a rising, which flows from the realization of the common good, the growth of the kingdom. There needs to be tomb-time allotted. We are a resurrection people, but there are dangers involved in pushing the resurrection too quickly, by not allowing people to make the transition spiritually, emotionally, and psychologically. Collaboration generates hope and hope generates faith. Those engaged in ministry in these parishes model enthusiasm, as they energetically go about the ministries they have found to be life-giving. And they do it all conscious that God's time isn't always our time. They do it with patience and prudence.

Multiple-parish ministry is not the ideal. But it is possible. It can lead to some amazing and wondrous communities. It strikes at parochialism. It demands sensitivity to the needs of others. It requires a mission-focused approach, and it demands adaptive work and collaboration.

8

Best Practices

MARK AND KATE

These "best practices" honor those parish leaders who are on the cutting edge of emerging models of pastoral leadership. They have taken the time—often through the school of hard knocks, trial and error, and with a lot of blood, sweat, and tears—to discern, with the help of the Holy Spirit, new ways of being and doing church. We are most grateful to the many pastors, parish life coordinators, pastoral ministers, business managers, educators, and other ministers who have shared their best practices with us. They have come up with innovative ways to make the best of what was probably a less than ideal situation.

We also give thanks to the Holy Spirit, who we know helped more than a few pastors along the way. We praise God for His continued presence to the U.S. church, stirring us to action, gifting us for mission, and blessing us with vision.

◇◇◇

Why Collect Best Practices?

We must confess that we really don't like the idea of best practices when it applies to ministry, and especially when it applies to multiple-parish ministry. Far too often, the people who are asked to do workshops that feature best practices come from parishes that are in an economically advantaged suburb, have three to four thousand families, with a staff of twenty-five, and one person who can work full-time providing the best practices. Multiple-parish ministries are seldom so advantaged. Staff persons who wear many hats are not affirmed or energized by hearing these best practices. Instead, they come away feeling guilty or sad because the best practices will probably never be possible in their parish setting.

It is difficult to compile best practices because of the incredibly diverse set of circumstances in multiple-parish ministry. Linkages differ in geography, cultures, the leadership skills of the pastor, economic and personnel resources, and the engagement of parishioners. A best practice in one place may not be applicable in another.

So with these caveats, we share with you the best practices of multiple-parish ministries that we have learned from parish leaders across the country. They may not be applicable to the multiple-parish ministry situation in which you find yourself. You may want to think of them not so much as best practices but as some pretty good ideas. If you find them applicable in your unique multiple-parish ministry situation, that's great. If not, then perhaps they can at least act as a catalyst or springboard for the in-breaking of the Holy Spirit to come up with an even better idea that will work in your unique setting.

What Makes a Best Practice?

The goal of best practices is not necessarily to reduce expectations, but to increase the number of resources. In other words, these best practices help the pastor place a higher priority on those activities that provide the most benefit for the expenditure of time and talent.

For example, a linkage has forty homebound parishioners, scattered across three parishes, who should be visited on a regular basis. For some pastors, this can be an overwhelming task, given travel time and time for the visit. A possible best practice here would be "multiplier ministry." This means that the pastor would recruit and train members of the parish to assist in outreach and visiting of the sick and homebound. Often the benefit/cost ratio is very good here. If the pastor invests five hours in training someone for this ministry, that person, in turn, should be able to visit more people, more often, than the pastor could by himself.

Having explained what we mean by "best practices," we'll explore some that have made a difference for the pastor, staff, and parish members. We've grouped these best practices into eight categories.

- Self-Care for Pastor
- Overarching Best Practices
- Building Inter-Parish Communication, Cooperation, and Community
- Councils and Committees
- Finances
- Worship and Sacraments
- Miscellaneous Best Practices for Parishes Sharing a Pastor
- Diocesan Best Practices Related to Parishes Sharing a Pastor

Self-Care for the Pastor

We start with the best practices for the pastor because the pastor is the key in linkages. There's a well-known refrigerator magnet that says, "If Mama ain't happy, nobody's happy." The well-being of parishes sharing a pastor depends on the well-being of the pastor. If that person is overwhelmed, unhealthy, resentful, ineffective, noncollaborative, or just plain unhappy, the people in the pews will feel it.

Self-care is not optional. It is not selfish. Multiple-parish ministry demands self-care of the pastor so that they can lead effectively. And that self-care should be comprehensive, encompassing their spirituality, their personal health and well-being, their ongoing formation, and their pastoral abilities and ministry. We will address each of these separately.

Spirituality

Pastors tell us that the best practice in the area of spirituality is simply making it a priority in your life. Schedule retreat time one year in advance, just as you would schedule vacation time. Schedule your prayer time on the calendar. Actually put it in your day planner. Prayer led you to this ministry; doing this ministry requires ongoing prayer. In addition, put in your appointment book at least one hour each week for quality personal prayer time or for spiritual reading.

Personal Health and Well-Being

Poor diet and neglect of exercise leads to burnout. Good nutrition and regular exercise can increase energy and help pastors handle the challenging day-to-day demands of multiple-parish pastoring. And when there is a more significant crisis that you are called to address, the extra energy in your system allows you to address the concern without wiping you out.

Every adult should have an annual physical. The stress of pastoring multiple parishes can have an adverse effect on your health. Therefore, a checkup is even more important for you than the average adult. Furthermore, it is also essential that when you do become ill that you care for yourself immediately, ensuring a more rapid and complete recovery.

Pastors throughout the project have told us that every pastor of multiple parishes must take time off, away from the ministry and the parish. It is all too common for busy pastors to skip regular days off each week or fail to schedule vacations. In countless forums, panelists acknowledged this ministerial trap and lamented how often it proved to be a one-way ticket to burnout, which, in the long run, served no one's interests or needs.

Ongoing Formation

The best practice for ongoing formation is to get a mentor. Look around in your diocese and find out who has experience in this emerging area of ministry. Offer to take them to the best restaurant in town, so that you can pick their minds and learn from their experience.

A second best practice is to get into a support group. In one diocese, a group of pastors who had two parishes each began getting together once a month. They gathered later in the afternoon for an hour of discussion, cocktails, and then had dinner together. Most found it to be critical to their success. In one particular diocese, someone came up with the idea to get everyone black T-shirts that had on the front of them "Father of Twins," which is not a bad image for the challenges faced by multiple-parish leaders. We applaud the sense of humor exhibited here; we firmly believe that laughter is the music of the soul.

These two best practices apply to other ministries, as well. Pastoral ministers, parish secretaries, directors of worship, directors of religious education, and business managers all benefit from mentor and support groups.

Pastoral Abilities and Ministry

Pastors should work from their gifts and manage their liabilities. Those in multiple-parish ministry regard this as essential. Each of us has been given ministerial gifts for the building up of the kingdom. Gifts are those aspects of the ministry that we look forward to doing, those things that we can do for hours. Each person in ministry has different gifts. For some, it might be pastoral care or teaching. For others it might be administration or outreach to the poor and needy. To increase the likelihood of success in ministry, a best practice would be to put as much time as you can into the areas of your ministry that engage your gifts, while minimizing the amount of time in those areas of ministry that tend to draw life out of you.

Fr. Hank was about to take on the responsibility of six parishes that had recently been linked together. He was very anxious about the challenge and came to me (Mark) for coaching and support. I asked him what his gift is, what part of his ministry he found most rewarding. This turned out to be youth ministry. However, he sadly noted that he had given this up years before, because there just wasn't enough time and he didn't want to infringe on the job responsibilities of the Director of Religious Education. I encouraged him to find a way to use this gift, and Fr. Hank eventually made a commitment to spend Tuesday afternoons during most of the school year as his sacred time to prepare for the classes he taught for the youth of his parish.

Then I raised the flip side of the issue. "What are the aspects of ministry that drain the life right out of you?" Without hesitation, he said, "Meetings, reports, administration." I wasn't surprised. I advised him to hire the best parish business manager that the parish could afford and to delegate to him or her as many of the meetings, reports, and administration as possible.

Fr. Hank did just what we discussed. His coping, problem solving, and energy levels were always their best when he knew that at least once a week he could look forward to that special time with youth. He found a capable parish business manager. As a result, Fr. Hank, in his own words, "spent seven of the best years of my ministry working with a team of ministers, each working out of their gift in service to the six parishes."

A second best practice is for the pastor to learn administration. Few priests receive any training in administration. Historically, priests learned administration by spending many years as an associate. Today, many priests are not mentored or apprenticed in the administration skills, and many struggle unnecessarily in this role. Research done by CPPCD in its reorganization study[66] indicated that when pastors take on two or more parishes, there is usually a significant increase in the amount of time the they will spend in administration.

Pastors are encouraged to learn administration even if they have a business manager. They will need to be able to supervise and give direction. The following are the areas of administration that we feel are essential for pastors:

Time Management: The art of setting priorities and structuring your time to make sure that you make progress in addressing those priorities

Personnel Management: Recruiting, hiring, training, mentoring, empowering, supervising, providing feedback, and, if necessary, terminating paid and volunteer staff.

Finances: Raising funds and using basic accounting to prepare and manage a budget.

Overall Administration: Pastoral planning, collaborative decision making, and establishing priorities.

Overarching Best Practices

While there are many specific ministry, organization, and program best practices, there are a few that cut across them all. We offer these before proceeding to more specific best practices.

Common Training and Continuing Education

Successful pastors in the multiple-parish ministry setting tell us that the recruitment, training, and empowerment of parishioners for various ministries are critical. They recommend conducting joint area trainings for catechists, lectors, acolytes, greeters, visitors for the sick and homebound, and lay presiders for word and communion services. They further recommend doing common training and orientation programs for new and continuing pastoral council members, finance council members, trustees, and members of parish committees for worship, education, social justice/concerns, stewardship, and evangelization.

Standardization

One of the obvious best practices is to get things standardized. Pastors regularly report that one of the biggest challenges in multiple-parish ministry is dealing with the unique and special ways that each parish does what it does. The stress of keeping it all straight can be considerable. We have seen the benefits of standardizing software, liturgy aides, electronic calendars, and other processes.

A word of caution: remember that standardization is not the goal; it is a means to an end. The end is to increase the effectiveness and efficiency of the work of the parishes. Standardization may be a legitimate means to that end, but consideration needs to be given to how it will impact the individual and the unique character and needs of each parish. Saving time, energy, and money sounds good, but not if it results in the withdrawal of the very people you are trying to bring into collaboration. Moving too quickly can foster resistance.

Pastors of two or more parishes always face the challenge of serving their broader community, while respecting the culture and traditions that have been handed down through the generations by those who have worshiped at the individual parishes.

Fairness is an issue when trying to implement standardization in multiple-parish situations. If the policies or programs selected are always those of parish A, you can expect resentment in parish B. This problem can be further exacerbated if parish A is the larger of the two parishes. Whenever you have a clearly larger parish linked with smaller parishes, the natural tendency of the smaller parishes is to fear that they may be ignored and eventually gobbled up by the largest parish. Hence, they are sensitive to the introduction of practices from parish A. They will challenge the process by asking why equal consideration is rarely given to things "that have worked for years" in the smaller parish. The best new programs are those that can integrate and take a little of the best practices of each of the parishes.

Keeping in mind these sensitivities on standardization, the following are the most common things that pastors standardize:

- Basic organizational policies and procedures
- Personnel and salary policies
- Accounting and database systems
- Worship practices and worship aids
- Missalettes and music books
- Operating guidelines for pastoral councils, finance councils, and committees

Common Calendar

Common calendars make the best practice list for multiple reasons. They facilitate cooperation and collaboration, they reduce competition, and they eliminate the need to "bi-locate." An up-to-date, inter-parish calendar that is readily accessible to all staff, parish leaders, and parishioners makes sense. You may even consider posting a version of the inter-parish calendar that anyone can view on a Web site. Common calendars for the pastor and staff should include:

- Mass schedules for weekend, weekdays, and holy days

- Basic schedule for the pastor, including parish meetings, vacation times, days off, and retreat times
- Significant, individual parish events
- Programming, such as religious education or sacramental prep times
- Parish meetings

Staff Meetings

In general, in the early stage of a new linkage, it is probably best to maintain existing staff patterns and structures. However, to limit the amount of time the pastor spends in staff meetings, joint staff meetings a few times per year with all staff together are recommended.

Staff Distribution

Over time, parishes may want to move toward a shared staff that has offices in one place, but serves two or more parishes. Pastors spoke frequently of the benefits of shared staff and centralized staff. Shared staff might initially include book-keepers and business staff, secretaries, maintenance staff, faith formation directors, directors of worship and sacred music, and pastoral ministers.

To help maintain parish identity, some multiple-parish pastors suggest maintaining at least a part-time secretary and office in each parish. The continued presence of a parish office is an important symbol for parishioners of the long-range viability of the parish. Other pastors prefer to consolidate parish offices and staff. However, distance between parishes may be an important factor.

The location of the pastor's residence and the location of the office and staff are important symbols. To help balance the distribution of these symbols, some in multiple-parish ministry place the staff in parish A, while the pastor lives in the rectory at parish B.

Building Inter-parish Communication, Cooperation, and Community

Much depends upon good working relationships within the linked parishes. Not surprisingly, a great number of best practice recommendations focus on building these relationships through good communication, cooperation and collaboration, and the establishment of community, rather than parochial, priorities. Following are recommendations aimed at doing these things.

Give Your Linkage a Name

Sharing a name and an identity unifies. It can even set the stage for the common mission. It encourages collaboration. It discourages competition. For all these reasons, giving the linkage a name ranks high among the best practices that lead to unity and growth. If all the parishes that are under a common pastor are in the same city, perhaps you could adopt "(Name of your city) Catholic Community Initiative," "The Catholic Community of (name of city)," or even "The Near East Side Catholic Community," etc. If the linkage covers a wider region, perhaps you could adopt a name such as "The (name of your county or region) Catholic Consortium" or "(Name of your county or region) Catholic Initiative."

Common Bulletin

Producing just one bulletin for parishes sharing a pastor saves money, eliminates duplication of effort, and builds better inter-parish communication. It is one of the most frequently recommended best practices. However, a word of caution: sensitivity is required. For many, the bulletin is a significant symbol of the regular communication, identity, and vibrancy of their individual parish.

The cover of a common bulletin should include the names, if not the pictures, of each of the parishes. Inside, it should have distinct and clearly delineated sections. First, there should be a section for information that is common to all the parishes— for example, a letter from the pastor, the Mass schedules, or the special programs open to all parishes. Next, there needs to be a section for information specific to each parish.

Common Web Site

Web sites are becoming an essential means of communication. Few small parishes have the resources or experience to run a good Web site. However, by working together and sharing expenses, the parishes in the linkage can have a common Web site. It would have individual parish information; but it would also be an effective tool for evangelization and welcome to those in the area who want to learn more about the Catholic faith and community in the area. Furthermore, a well-designed, engaging, informative, and up-to-date Web site can help reach youth and young adults.

Create New Events

Many parishes have one or two major festivals or fundraisers per year at which the majority of the parish turns out. Pastors should maintain these events out of respect for the individual parishes, but also develop something new. Possibilities include a new inter-parish annual festival, special outdoor Mass, picnic, auction, or fundraiser. These events engage the leadership and parishioners in all of the linked parishes and reinforce the need for collaboration and its benefits.

Create New Programs and Traditions

Affirm and maintain the important programs and traditions of individual parishes, but also develop some new ones. Some good examples of this include an annual Thanksgiving food or clothing drive or an annual banquet to honor the volunteers from all the parishes—you can even give out special awards, such as "Volunteer of the Year" or "Family of the Year."

Shares Spiritual and Catechetical Opportunities and Programs

Best practice lists always include collaborative spiritual and catechetical programming and opportunities. Lowering the cost is the least important reason for collaborative ventures. The programs and opportunities shared by linked parishes usually prove to be of a higher quality. Shared programs also contribute to the building up of community as members of each parish meet and come to know people from outside their parish.

The most common shared programs are those for youth, such as religious education programs, Confirmation preparation,

Teen Life liturgies, and youth ministry activities. But parishes might also want to consider programs for young adults, such as "Theology on Tap" retreats, and social events such as ski trips and special dinners.

Linked parishes might also have the resources to serve adults in new ways. Adults are hungry for formation and eager to come to know other adult Catholics who are practicing their faith. The best practice list for adults includes shared retreats, missions—with the first night in parish A and second night in parish B—and small faith-sharing groups.

Carpooling for Events and Training

Everyone knows that "everything happens at the See City," the site of the diocesan offices. While there is probably some truth to this, when this does happen, help to organize carpooling for parish leaders and parishioners, so that they can attend such events. This is a best practice because it promotes inter-parish relationships, more ministry, and program sharing.

Conference Calls

A best practice for easier communication is to make greater use of conference phone calls with people who are in different locations. A pastor might regularly schedule a conference call with the chairpersons of each of the pastoral or finance councils. Staff from the various sites can gather in their own offices, rather than drive to a meeting to consult on key pastoral or program matters.

Councils and Committees

Too many nights spent attending meetings can drain pastors. One pastor wryly noted, "God so loved the world that he didn't send a committee." However, another pastor shared, "Keep in mind, it was at a meeting that the Holy Spirit first came and changed the face of the earth." With these thought in mind, we offer a few best practices for councils and committees.

Councils Meeting Night

Pastors suggested the best practice of scheduling one meeting night at the same site for all parish pastoral and finance councils. Begin the evening with prayer, followed by a short agenda that includes announcements and issues common to all. Then have the councils meet separately to deal with concerns unique to their parish. The pastor and staff can roam from meeting to meeting, plugging in where needed or requested.

All Committee Night

This expands the council idea to include all parish committees. Start the evening in common prayer, announcements, and quick consultation on important parish concerns. Then split into various rooms to continue meetings. Pastors and staff can then plug in when needed. Consider having every committee take a common break. Keep it to fifteen minutes. This facilitates community building and more inter-committee cooperation. This model allows pastors to be more present to parish committees that they otherwise rarely have time for.

Inter-parish Councils and Committees

According to data by Sr. Katarina Schuth, only thirty-one percent of priests serving multiple parishes have organized inter-parish councils.[67] Within the Multiple Parish Pastoring Project, pastors, parishes, and diocesan staff noted the benefits of these councils. They help to facilitate inter-parish communication, coordination, and cooperation. They build community among the members, who are instrumental in bringing this sense of community to their respective parishes. They provide leadership within the linkage. They give the pastor a place to collaborate with that leadership, thereby avoiding the need for shuttling between pastoral councils.[68] Such bodies may meet on a monthly basis, quarterly, or even only twice a year.

Inter-parish Congress

Since the majority of linked parishes do not have inter-parish councils, pastors suggest organizing inter-parish congresses especially in those areas where parishes are widely separated geographically. Pastors invite all council and committee members to come together for either a full or half day once or twice a year. They celebrate liturgy together. They may include time for continuing education or enrichment with a speaker. The congress provides a forum for doing inter-parish calendaring, priority setting, and dealing with important inter-parish issues and concerns.

Finances

Financial issues need to be addressed quickly and fairly, especially in the initial phases of the linkage. More often than not, parishes that are assigned to share a pastor lack financial reserves and fear further financial strain as a result of the linkage. Participants in the Multiple Parish Pastoring Project recommended three best practices to assist in these financial areas.

Envelopes and Collections

Most parish linkages result in significant changes in Mass schedules, either through a reduction in the total number of Masses or changes in Mass times. This causes some parishioners to attend Mass at a parish other than their home parish. They worry about providing ongoing support to their own parish. If they put their envelope for St. John's in the basket at St. Mark's, where does the money go? What happens to their contributions?

Most multiple-parish linkages establish policies to deal with this concern. The policies ensure that parishioners are free to put their weekly offering envelope in the basket of any church in the linkage, and that the envelope will be returned to their home parish for deposit. Loose change gathered by the collection at Mass stays at the parish where it is collected.

It is helpful if the envelopes for each parish are unique in the choice of color or overall design. That makes them easier to pick out when sorting and counting a collection. Also, some pastors recommend expanding the coordination to include all the parishes within the area, not just those within the linkage.

Joint Purchasing

Joint purchasing provides a way of cutting expenses. Most supply costs can be reduced through bulk purchasing. Parishes that have begun this practice can purchase everything from appliances to computers, paper towels, and office supplies at a reduced cost. It requires coordination, but the time and energy spent have real, financial value.

Sharing Expenses

Pastors say that the best formula for sharing expenses is based on contributing units, the number of households who contribute $100 or more per year. Each parish's portion of the shared costs of clergy and staff salary is based on the number of registered households. One troublesome area is the cost of improvements to the house for the pastor. We recommend that those costs be paid entirely by the parish where the property is located, because it will be the benefactor in the end of any improved value in property. If there is a need to do fundraising for the project, the other parishes may be invited to help.

Worship and Sacraments

We are a sacramental people. The core of a parish is its worship and sacramental life. They shape the community, and the community expresses itself through them. Sharing a pastor impacts the worship and sacramental life of the faith communities involved. These are the best practices for this crucial area.

Major Celebrations

The location of the major celebrations of a parish matters to parishioners. When the seating capacities of the parishes are similar, the best practice is usually to rotate the site for major celebrations. Holy Thursday services are in parish A, Good

Friday in parish B, and the Easter Vigil in parish C. The following year you would change the locations for each of the services. The first year, when Holy Thursday is done in parish A, the service should be done sensitively and inclusively in the way parish A has traditionally done Holy Thursday services. The following year when Holy Thursday is done in parish B, it should likewise be done sensitively and inclusively in the way parish B has traditionally done Holy Thursday services. Seasonal penance services for Advent and Lent should also be rotated among the parishes.

If the seating capacity of the parishes is dissimilar, there is a tendency to choose the larger church for those celebrations of which there is only one annually (Holy Thursday, Easter Vigil, Midnight Mass on Christmas).

Parish Liturgy Coordinators

Someone other than the pastor needs to be responsible for the essential set-up, preparation, and coordination of the logistical and liturgical matters. Pastors say that it is a best practice to recruit and train a parish liturgy coordinator to do this. In some parishes, these individuals are called sacristans. They take responsibility for all sorts of details: that the church is open, that the heat or air conditioning is turned on, that there is enough altar bread and wine set out for the consecration, that someone is prepared to bring up the gifts, that all the liturgical ministers are present and accounted for (greeters, acolytes, lectors, extraordinary ministers of the Eucharist), and that the collection is taken care of following the liturgy.

Inter-parish Choir

One best practice with great potential is the development of an inter-parish choir for major holy days and inter-parish events. The choir allows ownership by all, regardless of where the celebration is taking place.

Lay Presider Training

Usually in linked parishes sharing a pastor, the number of weekday Masses is reduced. Depending upon diocesan policies and guidelines, word and communion services may be offered with deacons or lay persons as presiders. If this is the case in your linkage, those asked to preside should be provided with training.

Sacramental Preparation Programs

Sacramental preparation accounts for a huge investment of pastoral time. These are several best practices for this area.

Pastors recruit and train couples for baptism and marriage preparation. Often, the parishes combine preparation for these sacraments. Smaller parishes can rarely generate enough participation to warrant an RCIA process, but collaboration across parish lines can result in a thriving RCIA process led by a team formed from all the parishes involved. Formation and training are necessary.

Confirmation is the final area of sacramental preparation that frequently changes with a linkage of smaller parishes. An adult team of catechists and youth ministers should be recruited from all involved parishes. The youth supports such a program because the diversity of students adds interest and energy. If this approach is adopted, care should be taken to rotate the location of the celebration from parish to parish.

Common Song Books and Worship Aids

Implementing a common song book can be a fruitful collaborative effort. One pastor of four linked parishes began his ministry with each parish using a different hymnal. Each parish knew only one set of service music. After a year, he convinced the inter-parish council to look for common hymnals and missalettes. The inter-parish council researched and selected one hymnal and one missalette. All four parishes were provided with the new materials. In the long run, it generated more community, because when they gathered for special celebrations they were familiar with the songs and service music being used.

Miscellaneous Best Practices for Parishes Sharing a Pastor

Hire a Business Manager

Hiring a business manager to assist the pastor will pay great dividends The CPPCD study on parish reorganization noted that one of the most common changes in the lives of pastors, as they went from serving one to two or more parishes, was the significant increase in the amount of time that they spent in administration. Administration is the one thing that most pastors like to do least.

Justice, Fairness, and Stewardship Factors

From time to time, there will be conflict over proposed plans and changes. It is important for the pastor to take a step back and ask the following questions:

- Is the proposed action just and fair to all involved?
- Is what we are doing or proposing going to further the mission of the Catholic community in this area as a whole?
- Are we making the best use of talents, personnel, buildings, finances, and other gifts for the mission of the Church?
- If Jesus were listening to the discussion of the matter at hand and we asked for his advice, what might it be?

Diocesan Best Practices Related to Parishes Sharing a Pastor

The various participants throughout the Multiple Parish Pastoring Project offered some best practices for diocesan policies. They came from the pastors and also from the diocesan staff who worked in this field and had learned along with the pastor what worked and what didn't.

Lose Priest—Must Hire Staff Policy

A best practice is establishing a diocesan policy that says that when linking two or more parishes, funds previously allocated for the pastor must now go to the hiring of an appropriate staff. This is not a time for the parishes to cut personnel costs.

Provide Training and Mentoring

This emerging model requires training. A best practice is to develop training programs for pastors who serve multiple parishes. Only a small percentage of dioceses have developed such training programs.[69] Dioceses may also elect to send newly assigned pastors of multiple parishes to national training programs, such as the one developed through the Multiple Parish Pastoring Project. When formal training programs were not possible, dioceses developed and promoted mentoring programs so that those pastors who had served in this capacity could mentor those who were new to it.

Organize Peer Ministry Groups

Dioceses can foster peer support groups of pastors. This is one of the most frequently cited needs among pastors. This best practice could easily be organized by diocesan staffs who know the people involved. There is a need for, and interest in, multiple-parish ministry peer groups for pastors, parish directors, pastoral ministers, business managers, educators, and youth ministers.

Develop Weekend Help-Out Service

It is difficult for pastors to get help-out clergy so they can get away for vacations, retreats, weekend movement retreats, and take care of themselves when they are ill. Some dioceses have developed and coordinate a help-out service. When needed, a diocesan staff person makes the calls to secure help-out for pastors. In these cases, the diocese keeps an up-to-date listing of retired priests and those who are in specialized ministries, who may be available for service on weekends. We would like to encourage this as a best practice for dioceses, a real way to make a difference for those assigned to pastor multiple parishes.

Update Diocesan Policies and Programs

Most diocesan policies and programs are tooled for the "one parish, one pastor" model. Diocesan initiatives designed for single parishes can weigh down pastors of multiple parishes. Instead, dioceses should do what they can to affirm the heroic job that most pastors are doing in the face of monumental challenges and limited personnel and financial resources. Dioceses can be sensitive to the challenges and difficulties of multiple-parish ministry by updating their policies, procedures, guidelines, and manuals.

Assistance from Diocesan Staff

The service of an objective consultant and facilitator during the time of transitioning is critical. This consultant helps the pastor, parish leaders, and parishioners make decisions that will lead to smooth working relationships between the parishes, without creating unrealistic expectations that could lead to the burnout of the pastor. These consultants have the ability to ask the tough questions that need to be considered for the good of all.

Within the project, we heard the stories from pastors about the work being done on their behalf by diocesan staff working with them and supporting them through the transition period and beyond. We end with this best practice, because we feel it demonstrates how things can go when diocese, parish, pastor, and faithful work together to grow the church. It's collaboration at its best.

9

Where Do We Go from Here?

Some phenomenal pastoring is happening within these-multiple-parish situations. Through creativity, adaptive work, and collaboration, Spirit-led pastors, staffs, and parish communities are not only living their faith but growing the church.

Where do we go from here? First, we see signs of the Spirit's presence and of the Spirit's gifting of individuals and communities. We likewise acknowledge our dependence upon the Spirit's direction. We have seen the hand of God—the work of the Spirit—helping parishes to creatively adapt and grow through their less-than-ideal circumstances.

We wonder if these multiple-parish situations can serve as indicators of where the Spirit is leading the U.S. Church. Clearly, one indication is that we are being led into greater collaboration—clergy and lay, pastors and communities, parishes and dioceses. A second indication is that we are being led into a more mission-focused ministry that discourages parochialism and encourages the building up of the kingdom one community at a time.

There have been complaints, too. Individuals and communities say, "The church has put us in too tight a box; we can't make this work." We think that there is much more room for creativity and adaptive work than these dissatisfied individuals can see, or will admit. Helen Keller once wrote, "When one door of happiness closes, another opens; but often we look so long at the closed door that we do not see the one which has opened for us."

We have seen possibilities for greater collaboration between the pastors and staffs. We have seen their willingness to work through problems and give what it takes to make the situation work. We have seen pastors flourish as they minister pastorally to those entrusted to their care. The people involved in multiple-parish ministry situations that are thriving have taken their eyes off the door that closed, and have focused upon the one opened. They have labored charitably, with faith and hope.

We hope that this book and the resources available through the Emerging Models of Pastoral Leadership Project will prove beneficial to those who are entering the uncertain waters of multiple-parish ministry. We also hope that those who have been navigating in them for some time will find some new ideas. We recognize that no book can cover all the good ideas or practices from this emerging area of ministry. There is more to learn and more to share. But we have attempted to put forth the ideas that we believe have merit, and we look forward to continuing this process of learning and sharing in the future.

As we come to the end of this book, we wish to reflect on the challenges that have manifested themselves within this ministry. The situation leading to more multiple-parish ministries in the U.S. isn't going to change soon. In the near future we will see the retirement of some of our largest ordination classes, and we will be facing situations even more challenging than those today. But we believe that much can be done to ensure that the faith is learned, celebrated, and lived fully in parishes engaged in the multiple-parish pastoring model. As we bring this phase of the project to a close, we look ahead and ask the familiar question: Where do we go from here? We have five broad recommendations.

Training

A lot of training is needed. This was the number one recommendation from the April 2008 National Ministry Summit sponsored by the Emerging Models of Pastoral Leadership Project: *"Develop a comprehensive training program and materials for ministry in a multiple-parish environment for diocesan staff, pastors, deacons, parish life coordinators, parish staffs, lay leaders, parishioners, and seminarians."*

The pastors who are sent to minister to multiple parishes need training for the challenges of this ministry. If dioceses do not have such training developed and available, then we recommend that arrangements be made to send pastors to a national training program for multiple-parish ministry, such as the one offered by partnering organizations of the Emerging Models of Pastoral Leadership Project. This is especially necessary for those without much pastoral experience, the recently ordained, and especially those who are given multiple parishes as their first pastorates. Foreign-born priests who are responsible for more than one parish or mission would also benefit greatly from this training.

The staffs who serve in those parishes likewise need training for the special challenges they face. The lay leadership needs training to increase the effectiveness in their work on councils and in ministries.

Finally, the diocesan staffs responsible for implementing pastoral strategies and for supporting the pastor, staffs, and parishioners, need training so that they can assist more effectively and efficiently. They also need training to help them develop policies, programs, guidelines, and procedures that are appropriate for multiple-parish ministry situations.

Pastoral Planning

Our second recommendation resides in the area of planning. The need for pastoral planning was one of the major points raised in the April 2008 National Ministry Summit. Sr. Mary Montgomery, former director of Pastoral Services for the Archdiocese of Dubuque, used to tell the people in the parishes with which she worked, "If you don't plan for the future, you may not have one."

Reactive and ad hoc pastoral planning is inadequate. We recommend a proactive approach to the situation. While some situations can't be avoided because of unforeseen circumstances, many situations have early warning signs. Those in diocesan leadership are generally aware of the anticipated numbers of priests that will be available in the future. Planning for a future which will include fewer priests should be taking place in parish communities across the U.S. How are the communities going to continue? How can they work together to generate the most good? How will the work of the faith communities be accomplished? Who will be responsible for what? How can, and should, the clergy and laity collaborate to grow the church, taking into account the fact that there are fewer priests? What can the presbyterate within the diocese do to assist those called to multiple-parish ministry? What types of support need to be in place for these pastors?

Involvement and Support of Diocesan Offices and Staff

We have seen a real need for the involvement and support of the diocesan offices and staff during the transition to the multiple-parish model of ministry. That involvement and support needs to run the entire circuit: the beginning, the middle, and the ongoing phases. It needs to include personal presence to the pastor and the community. But it goes beyond that. This involvement also includes the development of policies, guidelines, and procedures that are tooled specifically for the multiple-parish situation. Involvement should include the development of best practices within the diocese, to affirm the good that is happening and also to provide examples for those who are just beginning. Finally, the offices and staff can be instrumental in organizing and supporting networking organizations for the pastor, the staff members, the parish council members, and the parishioners.

More Research, Discussion, and Exploration

To date, most of our research has focused on the pastor. While more research is needed in this area, the work of staff and parish members also needs study. The impact of multiple-parish ministry will be felt and lived for years to come. We need to better understand that impact. We need to identify more best practices so as to lessen the negative impact of this change. But more than that, we need to understand what has been effective in parishes that have grown, not just survived, through these situations.

In June of 2000, the USCCB Priestly Life and Ministry Committee released a "Study of the Impact of Fewer Priests on the Pastoral Ministry." This study, done by CARA, outlined the situation and measured the impact of fewer priests on priests, deacons, lay ecclesial ministers, and "the people in the pews." In 2006, the Multiple Parish Pastoring Committee, under the direction of the CPPCD and the NFPC through the Emerging Models of Pastoral Leadership Project initiative, sponsored a symposium on multiple-parish pastoring in the U.S. As we have noted, almost half of parishes and missions in the U.S. share a pastor and that number is expected to grow. We need to earnestly and honestly continue the discussion and exploration of multiple-parish ministry. We need to build on the good work already done. We need to invite to the table multiple-parish pastors and members of their staffs, diocesan staff members, pastoral planners, canonists, theologians, those in liturgy, education, social justice, and evangelization, clergy, deacons, social scientists, business leaders, and our bishops. We especially need the wisdom and guidance of our bishops as we take a stronger and more proactive approach to planning together for the future.

Celebrate the Good That Is!

Our final recommendation is to celebrate what is good. There is good happening within these multiple-parish ministry situations. Celebrate it, and let others know about it. Emphasize it in the bulletins. Speak about it from the ambo. Get a photographer out to capture an image of it for the diocesan newspaper. When we try to operate from a perspective of deprivation, we don't behave well. We hoard. We mope. We become territorial. We flare up over anything that resembles a threat. However, our behavior changes when we operate from a perspective of abundance. We share. We laugh. We build community. We see things for what they are. We may be facing some difficult challenges where the provision of pastoral care is concerned, but we are blessed beyond measure. We are moving forward in our mission. We are growing. The church in the U.S. is growing. Celebrate it.

In Conclusion

As we close, we know that we've only been able to scratch the surface of the exploration of multiple-parish ministry. Our hope is that this book will help to further the exploration and continue the discussion. Every day we hear of new, creative, and adaptive approaches to a myriad of multiple-parish situations and circumstances. We see this as the groaning and expression of the Spirit, alive and active in our church. As the church continues its journey, we look forward to walking with you.

Someone once made this tongue-in-cheek statement: "Believe it or not, now that you are in ministry, you will no longer have any problems. Instead, what you will face are opportunities for virtuous action! And there will be plenty of those." If you are involved in multiple-parish ministry, our hope and prayer for you is that God will be with you as you discern his will for yourself and for the communities you serve and that your opportunities for virtuous action will, in the end, be rich and rewarding.

Appendix A—Job Description for Pastor and Parish

The following responsibilities should be addressed in order to create a viable parish community. Items marked with an asterisk (*) must be the responsibility of a priest-pastor. Items marked with two asterisks (**) should have direct oversight by a priest. Other items can be delegated to properly trained, formed, and supervised laypersons.

Worship and Spirituality

Planning, coordinating the celebration of Mass, sacraments, the catechumenate

Work with liturgical committee or commission

Presiding/conducting

Weekend Masses*

Wake services

Wedding (priest/deacon)*

Baptism (priest/deacon)*

Funeral Mass*

Devotions/prayer services

Preaching (priest/deacon)*

Daily community prayer

Preparing people for sacraments

Care for the dying

Spiritual direction

Promote prayer, family prayer

Education and Formation

Planning, coordinating

Ensuring formation for all ages

Supervising

Training teachers and others

Teaching

Providing "vision"

Organizing Bible and other groups

Ensuring faithfulness in content**

Community building and leadership development

Promote parishioner participation

Develop, train parishioners for various roles

Evangelization, outreach

Personal presence at events

Develop social events for all ages, groups

Pastoral Care

Ensure/provide: **

Care of those in need

Counseling

General

Religious

Bereavement

Presence to parishioners: **

In times of crises

At special moments

Family ministry

Promote social action, social justice

Engage parishioners in mutual care

Administration

Lead pastoral and finance councils, ** in consultation/ collaboration with parish council, core staff

Personnel**

Hiring

Supervising

Developing

Planning

Ensuring financial management**

Ensuring care of buildings, assets*

Legal concerns*

Maintain records**

Ensure communication within parish, diocesan offices, other

Relation to Other Communities

Diocese

Deanery, vicariate

Committees, commissions

Continuing education

Personnel practices

Diocesan policies

Diocesan support

Bishop*

Ecumenical, ministerial associations

Civic, social structure

Appendix B—Summary of Pastoral Leadership in Multiple-Parish Ministry

Essential aspects of pastoral leadership in multiple-parish ministry include the following:

- **Mission focused:** Centered on Christ's mission
- **Adaptive:** Closing the gap between "what is" and "what is desired," because of the values held by the community through the intervention of the Holy Spirit
- **Accepting:** Managing the inevitable changes through visioning and discernment
- **Collaborative:** Engaging others in growing Christ's church

Skills that improve and enhance the ministry of pastors of multiple parishes include the following:

- Persons and leaders of prayer
- Transparency and openness
- Pastoral presence
- Pastoral planning skills
- Conflict managements skills
- Community building skills
- Ability to delegate
- Administrative skills
- Skills in personnel management
- Fiscal management skills

- Time management skills
- Communication skills
- Stress management skills
- Ministerial self care

Appendix C—
A Sample Planning Framework

This is a document used for the process of planning and implementing multiple-parish linkages in the Diocese of Green Bay, Wisconsin.

Definition of Linkage: When two or more parishes are served by one pastor or a team of several priests, one serves as the moderator. The parishes remain essentially separate, but may collaborate with other programs and ministries.

Decision-Making Process

The parishes involved in change have participated in area-planning studies.

Upon the departure of a pastor or parish life coordinator, the priest personnel board of the diocese determines whether to recommend to the Bishop implementation of linkage.

A member of the staff of the diocesan pastoral services department meets with pastor(s) or parish life coordinator(s) and pastoral council(s) with the following objectives:

- To present the recommendation for linkage and listen to parish leadership, in case there have been significant changes in the situation of the parish that warrant a re-evaluation of the recommendation
- To educate parish leadership in what it means to link the parish

- If needed, to set up open parish meeting(s), so that members of the parish will have an opportunity to learn what it means to link the parish
- To assist in the recruitment and organization of a transition task force, to develop plans for the implementation of the linkage, which would consist of representatives from the parishes and the remaining pastor or parish life coordinator

The transition task force meets and makes recommendations to the pastor or parish life coordinator and respective pastoral councils on how best to implement the linkage.

Transition Task Force

Makeup: The transition task force should be made up of the pastor or parish life coordinator who will serve the linked parish(es) and two or three lay representatives from each parish. At least one of the lay representatives should be a member of the pastoral council. A member of the staff of the diocesan pastoral services department is available to assist the work of the task force.

Responsibilities
- To help the new pastor or parish life coordinator gain a better understanding of the culture and needs of the respective parishes
- To assist the new pastor or parish life coordinator in the formulation of plans for the implementation of the linkage, which will be presented to the respective pastoral councils of the parishes involved for further consideration

Meetings and Terms of Service: Typically, a transition task force meets on a monthly basis, and will meet for three to six months—or until such time as the pastor or parish life coordinator can begin to rely more on the existing pastoral councils for further plan implementation and development.

Linkage Plan Topics
Basic Data

- Number of registered and contributing households
- Average mass attendance and seating capacity of church
- Annual number of baptisms, weddings, and funerals
- Number of students involved in religious education or school programs
- Overall has the parish grown, stayed the same, or declined in recent years
- Distance, condition of roads, and travel time between parishes

Culture and Identity of the Parishes

- What makes each parish unique?
- What is important to know about the history of the parishes?
- Are there any special customs, traditions, significant annual events?

Pastor or Parish Life Coordinator

- Unique gifts and talents
- Leadership style
- Hopes, dreams, expectations, concerns

Staff

- Must hire full-time person when the number of priests is reduced: explore roles, responsibilities for pastoral associate, deacon, business manager, etc.
- How will the pastor's or parish life coordinator's time and pay be allocated between parishes?
- Current paid or significant volunteer staff
- Job descriptions for all staff
- Existing system for staff supervision, meetings, annual reviews, etc.

Parish Organization
Pastoral council

- Organizational guidelines
- Parish mission statement
- Is it feasible to consider meeting on same night as other linked parishes?

Finance council and trustees

Worship

- Mass schedule: weekend, daily
- Easter, Christmas, holy days, etc.
- Worship committee
- Training and roles of liturgical ministers
- Music: cantors, musicians, choirs
- Devotions

Education

- Board or committee for Catholic education

- Religious education program/staff
- School(s)
- Youth ministry
- Adult education

Finances

- General financial condition of respective parishes including assets and liabilities
- Bookkeeping services and accounting system
- Determine how parishes will contribute to salaries, benefits, housing, etc., for the pastor, parish life coordinator, or other shared staff
- Have parishes annually met the bishop's appeal target and maintained support of area schools?

Buildings and Grounds

- Overall condition of buildings—any pending or anticipated renovation or repair needs?
- Rectories
- Residence of pastor or parish life coordinator
- Empty rectory—options for use
- Any long-range plans for renovation or expansion of buildings
- Do current facilities meet the needs of the parishes

Adjusting to Change

- Keeping parishioners informed and providing an opportunity for input, as needed
- Being aware of emotional grief processes that may accompany change

- Helping parishes realign expectations when it comes to the availability of the pastor or parish life coordinator
- Helping the pastor or parish life coordinator adjust to demands of multiple-parish ministry

Other parish committees, organizations, or groups

Diocesan Staff Assistance

Diocesan staff is available to consult and assist in each stage of the linkage process.

Note: In the Diocese of Green Bay, parish life coordinators appointed according to the provision of canon 517.2 have the title "Parish Director." The title "Parish Life Coordinator" was used in this appendix to be consistent with the title for this position used in this book.

Appendix D—A Model for Stress Management and Greater Effectiveness in Ministry

Each person in ministry has been uniquely called and gifted by God. Each person has been given gifts to help build the Christian community. To begin, look at your current position: affirm, name, claim, and get in touch with the most life-giving aspects of your ministry. List on a separate sheet of paper as many life-giving aspects as you can. Typically, these will be a reflection of the gifts with which you have been blessed. Here are some questions to help you name them.

- Which aspects of ministry do you most enjoy?
- Which parts of ministry do you find most life-giving?
- Which activities do you most look forward to?
- During which parts of ministry does the time just seem to fly past?
- What makes your heart sing?

If possible, ask those with whom you work and/or those who know you well to name the gifts that they see in you.

Conversely, there are probably aspects of ministry that you believe you have to do as part of the job, but would prefer not to. Take another sheet of paper and begin to list those. Here are some questions to help you.

- Which aspects of ministry do you find less than life-giving?
- Which parts of your ministry would you rather avoid?

- Which tasks seem to take forever to accomplish?
- Which activities do you dread?

Consider what your typical week looks like. Look at both lists and determine how many hours each week you spend on the items on the first list and how much time you spend on items on the second list.

Reflection

When we work or do ministry utilizing our gifts—those things we just listed—we can accomplish exponentially more than when we spend time in those activities that are not easily done, take more time, or might be considered weaknesses. The more we can focus our time and energy on our areas of strength, the more life-giving, Spirit-filled, and effective our ministry will be.

Being called to ministry is a gift and a challenge. For persons in multiple-parish ministry, the challenges can be considerable because of unrealistic expectations, which can be self-imposed or come from staff members, lay leaders, parishioners, the diocese, or the greater church.

When expectations are very high and the personal, spiritual, material, and physical resources are relatively low, the result is a "stress gap." If the stress gap is too wide, it can quickly lead to burnout of the minister. See the diagram below.

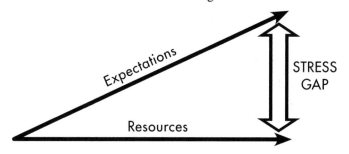

To close the stress gap, there are two options: reduce the expectations or increase the resources.

Step One: Clarify the Expectations: What Are They and Where Do They Come From?

List on a sheet of paper what expectations each of these has for you.

The church: What does the church teach about my role and responsibilities as a minister? What does canon law say? What do diocesan policies and standards say?

Lay leaders and parishioners: What do they expect from me as their pastor?

Staff: What are their expectations of me as pastor? How much time can I give to supervising and supporting staff? How can I be pastorally present for important programs?

Self: What do I expect of myself as a minister? What standards do I use to evaluate my effectiveness? My faithfulness? My successes and failures?

Step Two: Evaluate the Expectations

In light of the gifts, talents, and resources that you have, judge how to respond to these expectations. Which do you believe are realistic and which are unrealistic?

Those expectations that you believe are unrealistic offer you two choices when trying to close the stress gap. You can continue to tough it out, or you can enter into dialogue with the source(s) of those high expectations and try to lower them.

For example, parishioners can be led to modify an expectation that only a priest should visit those in the hospital.

Where possible, you can give yourself permission to not meet the expectation(s), thereby relieving some of the stress you feel.

Step Three: Increase the Resources Available to Respond to Expectations

Recruit and train, delegate and supervise—but don't abdicate responsibility.

In those areas of ministry that are less life-giving, try to recruit either paid or volunteer staff who you could train, delegate, and then supervise to respond to the expectations placed on you.

Work smarter through the use of best practices.

Spend more time doing ministry in areas that are life-giving and less time in areas of ministry that can drain life and energy.

Attend workshops, read, study, and learn best practices from peer groups that will help you to be more effective and efficient.

Tend to self-care—prayer, diet, exercise, sleep. A person who is physically, spiritually, and emotionally fit can accomplish considerably more than a person who is out of shape.

Stress Gap Management Worksheet

Source of expectations	Key expectations	Judgment: Realistic/ Unrealistic?	Can expectations be lowered?	Additional resources that could help	Best practices that could help
Church					
Parishioners					
Staff					
Self					

Notes

1. The six ministerial organizations collaborating in the Emerging Models of Pastoral Leadership Project are: National Association for Lay Ministry (NALM); Conference for Pastoral Planning and Council Development (CPPCD); National Association of Church Personnel Administrators (NACPA); National Association of Diaconate Directors (NADD); National Catholic Young Adults Ministry Association (NCYAMA); and National Federation of Priests' Councils (NFPC). The project was funded through the Lilly Endowment, Inc.

2. The survey was conducted for the Emerging Models Project by the Center for Business and Social Research at Loras College, Dubuque, Iowa, funded by Loras College, Kuchera Center, under the direction of the Multiple-Parish Pastoring Project Committee.

3. The best practices surveys and interviews were conducted by members of the Multiple Parish Pastoring Project Committee.

4. This preliminary study was conducted for the Emerging Models Project by Robert J. Miller of the Office for Research and Planning for the Archdiocese of Philadelphia.

5. A full report of the symposium's proceedings is available online at the Emerging Models Project Web site: http://www.emergingmodels.org.

6. The first, a one-day session held in the Diocese of Rochester, was sponsored by the pastoral planning offices of the Dioceses of Rochester, Syracuse, and Buffalo. The second, a two-day session held in the Diocese of Belleville, was cosponsored by the Dioceses of Belleville and Springfield. The two-day model proved to be vastly superior.

7. Taken from Emerging Models of Pastoral Leadership Project description, Emerging Models of Pastoral Leadership, http://www.emergingmodels.org/about.cfm (accessed January 1, 2008).

8. *Code of Canon Law*, Latin-English edition, new English translation prepared under the auspices of the Canon Law Society of America, Washington, DC, 2003, *Codex Iuris Canonici* (Vatican: *Libreria Editrice Vaticana*, 1983).

9. "Frequently Requested Church Statistics," *The CARA Report*, 13, no. 1 (Summer 2007): 6.

10. Ibid.

11. Katarina Schuth, *Priestly Ministry in Multiple Parishes* (Collegeville, MN: Liturgical Press, 2006), 3. Note that in Schuth's work, the term *parishes* combines those faith communities listed as "parish" and those listed as "mission" because of the variance in the application of the terms from diocese to diocese. CARA, in their research, limits *parishes* to those reported in that category by dioceses in *The Official Catholic Directory*.

12. This statistic is drawn from the national summary reports of selected volumes of *The Official Catholic Directory* (New Providence, NJ: P. J. Kenedy and Sons, 2000–2007).

13. Ibid.

14. These statistics are drawn from a comparison of the total Catholic population and total number of priests as reported in 1965 and 2007 volumes of *The Official Catholic Directory* (New Providence, NJ: P. J. Kenedy and Sons, 1965, 2007).

15. See report of study by Joseph Claude Harris, "Number of Active U.S. Diocesan Priests Expected to Decline 12 Percent by 2010," *The CARA Report*, 12, no. 3 (Winter 2007): 3.

16. Most notably Dean Hoge, *Future of Catholic Leadership: Responses to the Priest Shortage* (Kansas City, MO: Sheed and Ward, 1987) and Richard A. Schoenherr and Lawrence A. Young, *Full Pew and Empty Altars* (Madison, WI: University of Wisconsin Press, 1993).

17. The Conference for Pastoral Planning and Council Development (CPPCD) conducted and published two studies on parish reorganizations in response to the declining number of priests available to minister in parishes. See *A National Study of Recent Diocesan Efforts at Parish Reorganization in the United States: Pathways for the Church of the 21st Century* (Dubuque, IA: Loras College Press, 2004).

18. "The Study of the Impact of Fewer Priests on the Pastoral Ministry: Executive Summary," United States Conference of Catholic Bishops, June 2000, http://www.usccb.org/plm/summary.shtml (accessed December 30, 2007).

19. Schuth, *Priestly Ministry in Multiple Parishes*, 3.

20. Ibid., 182.

21. Ibid.

22. Mary Gautier, "Parishes Past, Present, and Future: Demographic Realities," in *Multiple-Parish Pastoring in the Catholic Church in the United States Symposium Report*, Emerging Models of Pastoral Leadership Project, http://www.emergingmodels.org/article.cfm?id=20 (accessed January 1, 2008).

23. This is in reference to cc. 519, 528, 529, 536–37, 545–48. James A. Coriden, *The Parish in Catholic Tradition: History, Theology, and Canon Law* (New York, NY: Paulist Press, 1997), 96–97.

24. John Paul II, *Christifideles Laici*, 26.

25. Benedict XVI, "Meeting with Clergy," *Origins* 37, n. 11 (Aug 16, 2007): 190.

26. Schuth, *Priestly Ministry in Multiple Parishes*, 21.

27. Ibid., 23.

28. National Pastoral Life Center (NPLC), "Alternative Staffing of Parishes," *Center Papers: A Resource for Diocesan Leadership* 3 (1987, rep. 1999): 11.

29. An initiative conducted by the Conference for Pastoral Planning and Council Development (CPPCD) in collaboration with the National Federation of Priests' Councils (NFPC) for the Emerging

Models of Pastoral Leadership Project funded by a grant from the Lilly Endowment, Inc.

30. Benedict XVI, *Spe Salvi*, 1.

31. USCCB, *Basic Plan for the Ongoing Formation of Priests* (Washington, DC: United States Catholic Conference of Bishops, 2001) Part One: E.

32. See Elisabeth Kübler-Ross, *On Death and Dying* (New York: Routledge, 1973) for a complete listing of the stages of grieving.

33. Luke 1:37.

34. Michael Weldon, *A Struggle for Holy Ground: Reconciliation and the Rites of Parish Closure* (Collegeville: Liturgical Press, 2004), 123.

35. See Appendix A for a list of issues to be negotiated by mediator at preliminary meetings.

36. Schuth, *Priestly Ministry in Multiple Parishes*, noted at the time of her research (2005) that "20 percent (4,408) of the 22,302 active priests serving in parish ministry had multiple-parish assignments" (page 3). Within the study, 92.1 percent of these priests served as pastors or administrators (page 181). CARA issued a special report in 2005, "Understanding the Ministry: Parish Life Coordinators in the United States," in which it reported that only 79 of the 566 (14 percent) of parish life coordinators in the U.S. were entrusted with the pastoral care of more than one parish (page 4).

37. The term "adaptive work" was developed by Ronald A. Heifetz in his work on leadership. See Ronald A. Heifetz, *Leadership without Easy Answers* (Cambridge: Belknap Press of Harvard University Press, 1994).

38. Siobhan Verbeek, JCL, "A Shepherd's Care: The Parish and the Pastors in Canon Law," in *Multiple-Parish Pastoring in the Catholic Church in the United States Symposium Report*, 9–13, http://www.emergingmodels.org/article.cfm?id=20 (accessed January 1, 2008).

39. Benedict XVI, "Meeting with Clergy," *Origins* 37, no. 11 (August 16, 2007): 190. While he is speaking of the pastors specifically, we

would add that what is being said applies to a great degree to parish life coordinators, too.

40. This ecclesiology of collaboration clearly flows from the Vatican II documents *Lumen Gentium*, *Gadium et Spes*, and most notably from *Apostolican Actuositatem* (2): "The Church was founded for the purpose of spreading the kingdom of Christ throughout the earth for the glory of God the Father, to enable all men [sic] to share in His saving redemption, and that through them the whole world might enter into a relationship with Christ. All activity of the Mystical Body directed to the attainment of this goal is called the apostolate, which the Church carries on in various ways through all her members. For the Christian vocation by its very nature is also a vocation to the apostolate. No part of the structure of a living body is merely passive but has a share in the functions as well as life of the body: so, too, in the body of Christ, which is the Church . . . the laity likewise share in the priestly, prophetic, and royal office of Christ and therefore have their own share in the mission of the whole people of God in the Church and in the world."

41. Ephesians 4:15.

42. Verbeek, *Multiple-Parish Pastoring Symposium*, 9–13.

43. Dean R. Hoge, *The First Five Years of the Priesthood: A Study of Newly Ordained Catholic Priests* (Collegeville, MN: Liturgical Press, 2002) and Katarina Schuth, *Priestly Ministry in Multiple Parishes* (Collegeville, MN: Liturgical Press, 2006).

44. Schuth, *Priestly Ministry in Multiple Parishes*, 192.

45. Benedict XVI, "Meeting with Clergy," 190.

46. See "Session III Discussion Outcomes: The Challenges and Opportunities of Multiple-Parish Pastoring," in *Multiple-Parish Pastoring in the Catholic Church in the United States Symposium Report*, Emerging Models of Pastoral Leadership Project, http://www.emergingmodels.org/article.cfm?id=20 (accessed January 1, 2008).

47. See Charmaine Williams, "Best Practices Regarding Multiple-Parish Pastoring," in *Multiple Parish Pastoring in the Catholic Church in the United States Symposium Report*, Emerging Models

of Pastoral Leadership Project, http://www.emergingmodels.org/ article.cfm?id=20 (accessed January 1, 2008).

48. John Paul II, *Christifideles Laici*, 26.

49. See Michael Cieslak's synopsis of the original research by Charlotte Haelhuhn and Len Decker titled "Multiple Parish Pastoring: Today's Realities and Tomorrow's Challenges," in *Multiple-Parish Pastoring in the Catholic Church in the United States Symposium Report*, Emerging Models of Pastoral Leadership Project, http:// www.emergingmodels.org/article.cfm?id=20 (accessed January 1, 2008).

50. See Michael Cieslak's synopsis of the original research by Jeff Rexhausen and CARA for the Conference for Pastoral Planning and Council Development (CPPCD) titled "A National Study of Recent Diocesan Efforts at Parish Reorganization in the United States: Pathways for the Church of the 21st Century," in *Multiple-Parish Pastoring in the Catholic Church in the United States Symposium Report*, Emerging Models of Pastoral Leadership Project, http://www.emergingmodels.org/article.cfm?id=20 (accessed January 1, 2008).

51. USCCB, *Coworkers in the Vineyard of the Lord* (Washington, DC: USCCB, 2005), 9.

52. Ibid.

53. David DeLambo, "A National Study of Recent Diocesan Efforts at Parish Reorganization in the United States: Pathways for the Church of the 21st Century," in *Multiple-Parish Pastoring in the Catholic Church in the United States Symposium Report*, Emerging Models of Pastoral Leadership Project, http:// www.emergingmodels.org/article.cfm?id=20 (accessed January 1, 2008). DeLambo reported that 74.4 percent of those in their first paid ministry position had been previously volunteering at the parish in which they were currently ministering. In addition, 50.8 percent had learned of their present ministry position through direct contact and recruitment by the pastors or other parish staff person. These statistics were drawn from his book *Lay Parish Ministers: A Study of Emerging Leadership* (New York, NY: National Pastoral Life Center, 2005).

54. DeLambo, *Lay Parish Ministers*, 19. In 2005, David DeLambo reported that there were 30,632 lay ecclesial ministers who worked at least twenty hours per week in paid positions in parishes. This number did not include those who work fewer than twenty hours or those who worked on a volunteer basis.

55. Second Vatican Council, *Apostolicam Actuositatem*, 10.

56. Schuth, *Priestly Ministry in Multiple Parishes*, 23.

57. Cieslak, "A National Study of Recent Diocesan Efforts at Parish Reorganization in the United States," in *Multiple-Parish Pastoring in the Catholic Church in the United States Symposium Report*, Emerging Models of Pastoral Leadership Project, http://www.emergingmodels.org/article.cfm?id=20 (accessed January 1, 2008).

58. Ibid.

59. DeLambo, "Lay Ecclesial Ministers," in *Multiple-Parish Pastoring in the Catholic Church in the United States Symposium Report*, Emerging Models of Pastoral Leadership Project, http://www.emergingmodels.org/article.cfm?id=20 (accessed January 1, 2008).

60. Cieslak, "A National Study of Recent Diocesan Efforts at Parish Reorganization in the United States," in *Multiple-Parish Pastoring in the Catholic Church in the United States Symposium Report*, Emerging Models of Pastoral Leadership Project, http://www.emergingmodels.org/article.cfm?id=20 (accessed January 1, 2008).

61. "Session I Discussion Outcomes—Parishes and Pastoring: Setting the Context," in *Multiple-Parish Pastoring in the Catholic Church in the United States Symposium Report*, Emerging Models of Pastoral Leadership Project, http://www.emergingmodels.org/article.cfm?id=20 (accessed January 1, 2008).

62. Loughlan Sofield and Carroll Juliano, *Collaboration: Uniting Our Gifts in Ministry* (Notre Dame: Ave Maria Press, 2000).

63. "Session V Discussion Outcomes—Models and Staffing of Multiple Parishes," in *Multiple-Parish Pastoring in the Catholic Church in the United States Symposium Report*, Emerging Models of Pastoral Leadership Project, http://www.emergingmodels.org/article.cfm?id=20 (accessed January 1, 2008).

64. Ibid.

65. DeLambo, "A Vision of Pastoral Excellence," in *Multiple Parish Pastoring in the Catholic Church in the United States Symposium Report*, Emerging Models of Pastoral Leadership Project, http://www.emergingmodels.org/article.cfm?id=20 (accessed January 1, 2008). Also see full article by David DeLambo at www.emergingmodels.org/article.cfm?id=27 summarizing the research in this area to date.

66. Conference for Pastoral Planning and Council Development, *A National Study of Recent Diocesan Efforts at Parish Reorganization in the United States: Pathways for the Church of the 21st Century* (Dubuque, IA: Loras College Press, 2004).

67. Schuth, *Priestly Ministry in Multiple Parishes*, 205.

68. Bob Miller, "Interparochial Pastoral Councils: An Emerging Model for Parish Consultative Bodies," 17, Emerging Models of Pastoral Leadership Project, http://emergingmodels.org/article.cfm?id=29.

69. Cieslak, synopsis of the original research by Charlotte Haselhuhn and Len Decker.

The Project: Emerging Models of Pastoral Leadership

One of the most significant challenges now facing the church in the United States is the diminishing number of priests available to pastor parishes. In order to ensure pastoral leadership of our parishes, the response most often chosen by bishops is to appoint one priest to act as pastor to several parishes at the same time. This emerging phenomenon, which is known as "multiple-parish pastoring," became one of the research areas studied by the Emerging Models of Pastoral Leadership Project. This growing phenomenon was studied under the guidance of a committee of veteran pastoral leaders chaired by Mark Mogilka. The committee developed a portrait of this emerging ministry and gathered information about what pastors need to be successful.

Those who have participated in these research initiatives have provided significant insight into this parish leadership model. We thank them for their contribution to the Emerging Models Project and for their contribution to shaping the future of parish life.

This project was part of a series of initiatives conducted from 2003 through 2008 by the Emerging Models of Pastoral Leadership Project, a collaborative effort of six national organizations funded by the Lilly Endowment, Inc., conducted national research on the emerging models of parish and parish leadership. The six partner organizations of the Emerging Models of Pastoral Leadership Project are:

- National Association for Lay Ministry
- Conference for Pastoral Planning and Council Development
- National Association of Church Personnel Administrators
- National Association of Diaconate Directors
- National Catholic Young Adult Ministry Association
- National Federation of Priests' Councils

Together, these six ministerial organizations conducted a series of research initiatives, including studies of lay ecclesial ministry, Canon 517.2 leadership, multiple-parish pastoring, human resource issues, the next generation of pastoral leaders, and best practices for parishes and parish leaders. Information on each of these initiatives is available on the Emerging Models Project website at www.emergingmodels.org.

Marti R. Jewell
Project Director

About the Authors

Mark Mogilka is the Director of Stewardship and Pastoral Services for the Diocese of Green Bay, Wisconsin. He is a national speaker and organizational consultant in the areas of pastoral planning and multiple-parish pastoring. He chairs the national study committee on multiple-parish pastoring for the Emerging Models of Pastoral Leadership Project.

Kate Wiskus currently serves as faculty and associate dean of formation at Mundelein Seminary/University of St. Mary of the Lake in Mundelein, Illinois. She served as director of pastoral services for eight years in the Diocese of Madison, Wisconsin, and currently teaches classes in multiple-parish pastoring. Her doctoral project and thesis focused on the pastors of multiple parishes.

Also available in the series:

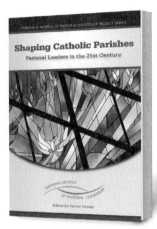

Shaping Catholic Parishes
Pastoral Leaders in the 21st Century

Twenty-two priests, deacons, religious, and lay people share first-person accounts of their experiences with new organizational models in the church.

2646-5 • 192 pages • $11.95

Parish Life Coordinators
Profile of an Emerging Ministry

This book explains how the PLC model works, shares best practices from parishes using the model, and offers practical implementation ideas.

2648-9 • 120 pages • $11.95

Both books are available in your local bookstore or by ordering direct.

Upcoming releases:

+ a book on the next generation of pastoral leaders and their interest in ministry. Written by Dr. Dean Hoge and Dr. Marti Jewell, this book is a must-read for all who work with recruiting and forming young people for ministry.

+ a book by David Ramey and Dr. Marti Jewell featuring the best ideas, initiatives, and practices of vibrant parishes and visionary pastoral leaders around the country. More than 500 leading-edge, grassroots pastoral leaders share groundbreaking thoughts on ministry, leadership, and the future of parish life in the United States.

For more information about these and other books in the Emerging Models of Pastoral Leadership Project series, **visit www.loyolapress.com/store**

LOYOLAPRESS.
A JESUIT MINISTRY

EMERGING MODELS
OF PASTORAL LEADERSHIP